"I stand here today, grateful for the diversity of my heritage, aware that my parents' dreams live on in my two precious daughters," Obama said to a hushed crowd.

"I stand here knowing that my story is part of the larger American story, that I owe a debt to all of those who came before me, and that, in no other country on earth, is my story even possible."

At first, many in the crowd wondered who this tall, thin man with the funny name might be. But as Obama told the story of his unusual background and how, because of the freedoms and the greatness of our country, he was able to make his hopes and dreams come true, the crowd became electrified. No one had ever seen a politician quite like him before.

**A Background Note about**
*A DREAM FULFILLED:*
*The Story of Barack Obama*

When Barack Obama was only six years old, he wrote his first essay titled, "I Want to Become President." This was a pretty big ambition for a first-grader, but young Barack enjoyed writing about it so much that he wrote another essay in the third grade with the same title. Actually, Barack simply loved to write. He continued keeping journals for years, often writing what he jokingly called "very bad poetry" along with outstanding prose.

Today, when we think of Barack Obama, we think of the young man who traveled an unlikely road to become our nation's 44th president and our first African American president. However, he should also be thought of as an accomplished and fascinating author.

Obama's two books, *Dreams from My Father* and *The Audacity of Hope*, have sold millions of copies worldwide. People particularly like *Dreams from My Father* because it is the exceptionally honest and moving story of Obama's search for himself during his youth and young adulthood. If you are interested in the life of the young Barack Obama (as millions of people have proven to be), you will definitely want to read *Dreams from My Father* after finishing this book.

# A DREAM FULFILLED

★ ★ ★

## The Story of Barack Obama

TANYA SAVORY

 THE TOWNSEND LIBRARY

# A DREAM FULFILLED
## The Story of Barack Obama

**TP** **THE TOWNSEND LIBRARY**

For more titles in the Townsend Library,
visit our website: www.townsendpress.com

Illustrations © 2010 by Hal Taylor

**Townsend Press, Inc.**
**439 Kelley Drive**
**West Berlin, NJ 08091**
**cs@townsendpress.com**

ISBN-13: 978-1-59194-186-6
ISBN-10: 1-59194-186-5

Library of Congress Control Number:
2009927414

# CONTENTS

# CHAPTER 1

In 1952, a ten-year-old girl named Ann Dunham invited a friend to come to her house to play. It was a warm October afternoon in the Texas town where Ann lived, so she and her friend decided to play in the front yard beneath a big maple tree that had just begun to turn gold. The two girls brought one of Ann's favorite books and sat down on a blanket in the cool grass, their heads bent together over the pictures in the book. One of the pictures made both girls laugh out loud, but their laughter died quickly as a sharp voice shouted at Ann from the street.

"Dirty Yankee!"

Ann and her friend looked up to see a small group of children from Ann's school gathered just outside the fence. The children were glaring at the two girls in disgust and pointing at Ann's friend, who was black. None of the children had ever seen a black child playing in their neighborhood before.

As all the children began shouting, Ann and her friend crouched low to the ground,

1

trembling in fear. One of the older boys began throwing rocks at the two girls while the rest of the group hurled insults. At that moment, Ann's mother, Madelyn, came walking down the sidewalk toward the house. When she approached, the group of children quickly disappeared. Madelyn Dunham shook her head, sighed, and walked over to her daughter and her daughter's black friend and rested her hand on both of the girls' heads.

"If you two are going to play, then for goodness sake, go on inside. Come on. Both of you."

Ann stood up to follow her mother, but Ann's friend, still shaking, took off without a word, running down the street as fast as she could. She never even looked back.

That evening, Ann's father, Stanley, became furious when he learned that a group of children had shouted racist remarks and thrown rocks at his daughter and her friend. Neither Madelyn nor Stanley had been raised to judge others based on skin color, and they weren't about to let their daughter get picked on just because her friend was black. It was not uncommon in 1952, particularly in Southern states, for black people to be treated like second-class citizens. They were often forced to use separate bathrooms, drink from separate water fountains, and sit in a separate section in the back of a bus. Quite often, blacks were prohibited from even entering certain restaurants, theaters, or stores. But Stanley and Madelyn knew this was wrong, and they had always taught Ann that it was wrong too.

The next morning, Stanley Dunham called the parents of the schoolmates who had been taunting Ann and her friend. Surely, the adults would see that this kind of behavior was wrong and that their children should be punished. In call after call, however, Stanley got the same responses.

"You best talk to your *own* daughter, Mr. Dunham. White girls don't play with coloreds in this town."

• • •

Half a world away, in the country of Kenya on the continent of Africa, a sixteen-year-old boy tended his father's goats in the late afternoon. The boy and his father, named Onyango, belonged to the Luo tribe. They lived in thatched mud huts not far from the shores of Lake Victoria, and they often wore no more than a broad piece of leather tied around their waists as they walked behind their herds of sheep and goats. The boy's father had three wives, something that was common in many African countries.

The boy attended a local school that had been set up by the British, the people who ruled over Kenya. Quite often the British treated the native Kenyans unfairly, in much the same way that Americans mistreated black people. However, some British people tried to help the Kenyans by setting up schools so that the young people could obtain the education they'd need to create better lives than their ancestors had experienced.

"Knowledge is the source of the white man's power," Onyango would often tell his son. Again and again, Onyango told his young son that he needed education if he wanted to succeed.

The boy knew his father was right, and even though the boy made excellent grades, he found it hard to stay out of trouble. Again and again, he was sent home for cutting up in class and rebelling against the school rules. Perhaps the boy sensed that all his studying and good grades wouldn't really make any difference. How would his hard work ever change anything? After all, the world around him made it painfully clear that a black man would never achieve greatness. That sort of thing was reserved for white men. Or perhaps the boy was bored. He often complained to his father that he already knew more than his instructors.

In time, the boy was expelled from his school. Onyango was so angry that he told his son that he was going to send him far away to work as a clerk for an Arab merchant. Onyango felt that his son had ruined his chances to be any more than just another black man working for someone else, and now he would punish his son by showing him what life was like in the real world.

The boy stood out on the wide savannah watching the sun set and listening to the tinkle of the bells around the goats' necks. On the horizon, a herd of zebra moved cautiously through the tall grass, wary of the hunting lions. Closer to the boy, high up in a huge baobab tree, a stork protected its young from a circling eagle. Every animal had its place, the boy thought. Perhaps that's just the way it was for him, too. Maybe it was wrong to want more.

But as the boy made his way back to the mud hut in his tribe's village, he knew in his heart that he had the power to make his life different and better—to become the change he wanted to see. And though he would leave tomorrow for a life he didn't want, he made a promise to himself that one day he would become a great man.

• • •

Eight years passed. Eighteen-year-old Ann Dunham had moved with her parents to Hawaii, an exotic place that had just become part of the United States. Ann's parents preferred the more open-minded and laid-back attitudes in Honolulu. Unlike many of the states in the United States in 1959, Hawaii did not tend to discriminate against minorities as much; there was more of a "live and let live" attitude.

As for Ann, she had hoped to attend the University of Chicago, but her parents told her that Chicago was too far away (4300 miles!) from home for an eighteen-year-old. As a result, Ann settled into her freshman year of college just down the street at the University of Hawaii.

At the same time, the boy from Kenya, who was now a twenty-four-year-old man, had kept his promise to himself. He had worked very hard to get back on track with his studies, and he had finally graduated from high school with excellent grades. His next dream was to attend college. As the son of a tribesman in a remote part of Kenya, the young man had no money and no connections to universities. But he had heard that some universities in the United States offered scholarships to foreign students, so he sent out letter after letter explaining his situation and asking politely for help. Soon the copies he kept of these letters filled an entire box.

Months went by, and no universities responded. Then, one spring afternoon in 1959, a letter reached the young Kenyan. A university in the United States was willing to pay his full tuition and expenses! In fact, the school explained that it would be proud to welcome him as their first-ever African student. Overjoyed, the young man rushed to get ready, and in only two weeks, he was aboard a jet for the first time in his life—a very long flight to Honolulu and the University of Hawaii.

• • •

Ann Dunham had noticed the student from Kenya in her Russian language class right away. He was tall and handsome and always at ease. Certainly he must have felt awkward at times in such a different culture, but he never showed it. He was also brilliant and funny, his jokes and sharp sense of humor making him many friends, including Ann. However, before long, Ann and the Kenyan became more than just friends. They fell in love and, rather quickly, decided to get married.

In 1960, it was still illegal in many parts of the United States for a black man and a white woman to marry. In some places, black men were threatened and even beaten merely for flirting with white women. Luckily, attitudes were not so strict in Hawaii. No one seemed too concerned about the young couple as they walked along the wide beaches, hand in hand. And when Ann told her parents that she wanted to marry her Kenyan classmate, they were happy for her.

In Kenya, however, Onyango was not at all happy with his son's decision. He worried that Ann would never move to Kenya and live the life of a Luo tribeswoman. He was concerned that Ann would not allow her husband to have multiple wives, something that was both a tradition and an expectation within the Luo tribe. Most of all, Onyango was angry that his son was deciding for himself whom he would marry. For generations and generations, Luo parents had arranged their children's marriages. A son deciding for himself was unheard of.

Nonetheless, Ann and the young man from Kenya would break with both United States and Kenyan traditions and get married in 1960. Then, in 1961, Ann gave birth to a baby boy. The child had his mother's eyebrows and sparkling eyes, but he had his father's broad smile. And he had his father's name: Barack Hussein Obama.

• • •

When Barack was very young, his father decided to attend graduate school in Boston, Massachusetts. Ann was not happy with her husband's decision. After only two years of marriage, Barack Sr. would be leaving Ann and their young son for a school thousands of miles away. He had done so well at the University of Hawaii that he had been offered two scholarships: one to a school in New York City, which would pay his entire family's expenses, and another to Harvard University in Boston, which would pay only his own expenses.

Again and again, Barack Sr. explained to Ann that it was very important to him to show his relatives in Kenya that he had received the very best education possible in the United States. Everyone had heard of Harvard. Going to this famous university would be his way of proving to his family that he had done his best.

And so, in the fall of 1963, Ann and two-year-old Barack waved farewell to Barack Sr. Perhaps Ann knew in her heart that their separation was the beginning of the end. Or perhaps it was Ann's mother, gently warning her daughter about the many violent uprisings in Kenya and how dangerous life there might be, that led Ann to question her marriage. Whatever the reasons, Ann and Barack Sr. divorced before the end of the year. Before young Barack was even old enough to have any memories of his father, his father was gone.

• • •

"Absolutely not," Madelyn Dunham, Ann's mother, said with a smile she was trying to hide. "I am *much* too young to be called 'Grandma.' You had better think of something else for Barry to call me. 'Grandma' is out of the question."

"Well, he's already calling me 'Gramps,'" Stanley Dunham shouted from the kitchen. "I'd vote for 'Granny' for you."

Madelyn Dunham looked at Ann and Barack, who had been nicknamed 'Barry' by his mother, and shook her head and rolled her eyes.

"I know," Ann finally said. "How about 'Tutu'?"

*Tutu* was the Hawaiian word for "grandparent," and Madelyn thought it was perfect. Young Barry, however, found it easier to simply say "Toot." It was a name that would stick, and for the rest of Madelyn and Stanley's lives, Barry would call them Gramps and Toot.

Because Ann was both working and attending college, Barry spent a great deal of time with his grandparents. Gramps would let Barry tag along when he went to a local park to play checkers or to the corner fish market to buy fresh tuna and salmon for the sushi they would often have for dinner. Once, before the sun had even come up, Gramps woke Barry and took him down to the docks near the beaches of Waikiki to go out on a fishing boat. In the pre-dawn gloom, Barry watched divers disappear into the black water and then reappear with huge rainbow-colored fish on the ends of their spears. Gramps told Barry that the Hawaiian name of the fish was *humu-humu-nuku-apuaa*, a name that, of course, sounded hysterically funny to five-year-old Barry. For the entire drive back home, Barry and Gramps repeated the name of the fish to each other, laughing until tears rolled down their faces.

For all the lighthearted fun Gramps had with his grandson, he knew that life would not always be so easy for a child who was half black and half white. In 1966, when Barry was five, the civil rights movement was in full swing. In Alabama, hundreds of black people marching for the right to vote had been injured by angry white police officers. The officers had used tear gas, fire hoses, clubs, and even whips in an attempt to break up what had been a peaceful march. And across the country, in Los Angeles, bloody and even deadly rioting erupted when the black community reached the end of its patience with white police officers' mistreatment of black people. After enduring more than three hundred years of injustice and cruelty, black people were fighting for their rights. The time for change had come, but many white people stubbornly and angrily swore that they would never allow it.

Hawaiians, in general, were neither racist nor bothered by the idea of black people having the same rights that white people had. Gramps's friends loved Barry and never thought less of him because of his racially mixed background.

But tourists to Hawaii were, quite often, not so kind. Gramps would notice white tourists glaring at the young black boy playing in the sand on some of Honolulu's fanciest beaches. *What is* he *doing here?* their expressions seemed to say. *He shouldn't be allowed!*

At times like these, Gramps loved to wander over to the tourists and, in a low voice, tell them that the boy they were watching was the great-grandson of King Kamehameha, the first ruler of Hawaii. Instantly, the tourists would scramble for their cameras, taking picture after picture of Barry as Gramps covered his grin with his hand.

"I'm sure that your picture's in a thousand scrapbooks, Barry," Gramps would often tell his grandson with a booming laugh. "All the way from Idaho to Maine!"

Barry giggled at the idea of being in strangers' scrapbooks, and Gramps smiled back. However, Gramps knew the day would come when he would no longer be able to shield his grandson from racism.

# CHAPTER 2

"**Y**our father was a terrible driver. He'd end up on the left-hand side the way the British drive." Ann was adding to a story that Gramps and Toot were telling Barry about his father. On a beautiful summer day, Barack Sr., Ann, Gramps, and Toot had taken a drive up a very steep and winding road to the top of a mountain. Along with them was a friend of Barack Sr.'s who, according to Toot, looked more frightened than anyone else.

Gramps went on to tell how, when they reached the peak, Barack Sr. had pulled out a pipe that he was very proud of and puffed away as the group looked at the view far below. At one point, Barack Sr.'s friend asked if he could try out the pipe. After only one puff, the friend began coughing so hard that he accidentally dropped the pipe. It fell one hundred feet down the side of the cliff.

"That's when your dad picked him clear off the ground and started dangling him over the railing!" Gramps told six-year-old Barry, laughing and slapping his knee. According to Gramps, Barack Sr. justified his actions by saying matter-of-factly, "I only wanted to teach the chap a lesson about the proper care of other people's property."

While the adults laughed at this memory, Barry looked with amazement at the pictures of his father on his grandparents' bookshelf. In Barry's mind, his father was a larger-than-life hero. Imagine being able to pick up a grown man and dangle him in the air just to teach him a lesson!

There were many other stories. Once, when Barack Sr. and Gramps had gone into a bar for a beer, a man sitting at the bar had looked right at Barack Sr. and told him that he didn't think black people should be allowed in the same establishment with white people. Instead of getting angry, Barack Sr. had sat down next to the man and launched into the history of racism, his belief in the rights of all humans, and the idea that the American Dream was a dream for all people of all races. By the time Barack Sr. finished, the man at the bar was so impressed and moved that he gave Barack Sr. one hundred dollars.

Then there were stories about how many friends Barack Sr. made, how he could handle any situation, and how brilliant and hardworking he was. There was even a story about his showing up at a big music festival and, on the spur of the moment, agreeing to sing some African songs for the huge crowd. With no band and no one else singing with him, Barack Sr. had stood on the stage alone, belting out songs and smiling his broad smile.

"Now *there's* something you can learn from your dad," Gramps would tell Barry. "Confidence. That's the secret to a man's success."

No doubt, Barry was impressed by the father he had never known. It seemed his father could do no wrong, and no one ever said a bad word about him. Still, questions nagged at Barry. What was his father doing now? Did his father ever think about him? And, most troubling of all: if his father was so great, why had he left?

• • •

The summer before Barry began grade school, he and his mother moved halfway around the world to Jakarta, Indonesia. Ann had met a young Indonesian man named Lolo as she was finishing her studies at the University of Hawaii, and, as she had done with Barack Sr., she fell in love and quickly married. This time, however, she agreed to follow her new husband to his native land.

Gramps had read that there were tigers and headhunters in Indonesia, a fact he brought up several times when trying to persuade his daughter not to move. In addition, Toot pointed out that the foods people ate in Indonesia might not be fit for a growing boy. After all, she had heard that some Indonesians even ate bugs.

Ann, however, assured her parents that she and Barry would be safe from wild animals, savages, and strange foods. While Ann's parents were not thrilled with her moving to Jakarta, she was too old to be told what to do. As the summer neared its end, Ann and Barry boarded a jet for the very long trip to Indonesia.

To Barry, Jakarta was a mysterious and exotic wonderland. Giant trees towered over small villages that disappeared into forests thick with bamboo. Strange, colorful birds filled the air; and people bathed, drank, and washed their clothes in the same rushing river that spilled out of a tall volcanic mountain. In Lolo's backyard were cockatoos, chickens, dogs, and even two baby crocodiles. Best of all, Lolo had a surprise waiting for Barry: a big pet ape named Tata. On that first evening, Lolo took Barry out to the yard to watch the beheading of the chicken they would be eating for dinner. For a few seconds, the headless chicken ran around in wild circles, flapping its wings and spurting blood. If Barry had been worried that life in a new land would be dull, his worries were gone before the day ended.

Because Lolo and Ann didn't have the money to send Barry to the special school for foreign students, Barry attended the local grade school. From the start, he enjoyed learning—particularly writing. In first grade, he wrote an essay titled, "I Want to Become President." Two years later, in third grade, he completed an assignment called "My Dream: What I Want to Be in the Future" with another description of how he would become a president. Barry's best friends were the sons and daughters of farmers and servants, children who nicknamed Barry "Curly Eyelashes" because of his long, dark lashes. They taught Barry how to make a kite, find odd jobs for pocket change, and eat dog meat, snake meat, and roasted grasshoppers.

As exciting as life was for Barry, his mother worried about his education. She felt he wasn't learning enough, so she ordered lessons from a United States correspondence course. Every morning at four o'clock, Ann would drag Barry out of bed to teach him his lessons for three hours before he left for school and she left for her job at the U.S. Embassy. Barry often complained, thinking up every excuse imaginable to avoid the lessons, but Ann was firm.

"This is no picnic for me either, Buster," she would often say when Barry would complain that he couldn't keep his eyes open.

After school was over, Ann frequently took Barry to the Embassy library so that he could study or browse through books. More often than not, however, Barry preferred looking through magazines and finding unusual pictures, trying to guess what the caption beneath each picture might say before reading it. One warm spring afternoon when Barry was about 9, he came across a picture of a man who looked like a ghost. The man's skin was a sickly shade of white, an unnatural color. Then, looking more closely, Barry was surprised to see that the man had a nose, lips, and hair like Barry's own.

Barry could not imagine what the caption would be, but when he read it, he was shocked. The man was a black American who had paid to have a chemical treatment that would turn his skin white. He had hoped to pass himself off as a white person so that he would be treated better, but he found out too late that the treatment would not "make" him white. Across the United States, thousands of other black people had paid good money to make the same horrible mistake.

Barry sat very still. In the quiet of the library, he could hear his heart pounding. Suddenly, Barry wondered if it was bad to be black. Would being black make people dislike him? It was, perhaps, the first time he had ever thought of himself as being different in a way that was bad. Growing up, of course, he was aware that he *looked* different from Gramps, Toot, and his mother; but he knew that his father was African, so of course his skin was darker, and his facial features and hair were different. He'd never thought too much about it beyond that. But now, a thousand questions filled his head. Barry took one last look at the ghostly black man and then slammed the magazine shut. That night he stood in front of the bathroom mirror staring at his own face, wondering, for the first time, if there was something wrong with him.

• • •

The summer before Barry entered fifth grade, his mother told him that she thought it would be best if he returned to Hawaii so that he could get a better education. She told Barry that Gramps would help him get into Punahou Academy, one of the best schools in Hawaii.

Barry wasn't sure how he felt. He had friends in Jakarta, not to mention a pet ape. He was growing closer to Lolo, the only father he had ever known. Lolo had taught him how to box and how to be brave even when he was frightened of something.

Ann pointed out, however, that Barry would no longer have to get up early in the morning to do extra lessons. Barry considered this briefly and then agreed that returning to Hawaii would actually be a great idea. Ann promised her son that she and Maya, Barry's new half-sister, would return to Hawaii before too long to visit him. One day, she assured him, they would all be together again for good.

Gramps and Toot met Barry at the airport, amazed by how much he had grown in four years. To Barry, Gramps and Toot hadn't changed much at all; but now, due to Gramps losing his job, they lived in a small apartment instead of their old house. Gramps worked at home trying to sell insurance, something he was not particularly thrilled with. Sometimes, at the end of another frustrating day, Gramps would remind Barry how important education was and how Barry could actually have a career he loved if he stayed in school and did well.

Punahou, a private K-12 academy, was quite difficult to get into, but Gramps had friends and connections at the school. After Barry went for some admissions interviews, the school gladly accepted him. As Gramps walked Barry through the grounds, he pointed out the incredible track and field facilities, the gardens, the tennis courts, and even a swimming pool. However, Barry was more concerned with making new friends than anything else. More self-conscious than the little boy who had left Hawaii years ago, Barry now worried that his new schoolmates would not accept him. Perhaps they would think it was bad that he was black.

• • •

"Barack? Barack Obama?" Miss Hefty, the fifth-grade teacher called the roll, using Barry's real name instead of his nickname. Barry fidgeted as the roomful of ten-year-olds giggled and turned to stare at the new student with the funny name.

Miss Hefty looked disapprovingly around the classroom and then turned to smile at Barry. "Your grandfather tells me that your father is Kenyan. Do you know what tribe he's from?"

With this question, the class burst into laughter, and one boy in the back made noises like a monkey. Barry could not have imagined a more horrible way to start his first day at Punahou. Still, he tried to be brave.

"Luo," Barry responded nervously.

More laughter and monkey noises.

Miss Hefty glared at the students and then went into some detail about how beautiful Kenya was and how she had actually taught there some years ago. As some of the students still snickered, Miss Hefty paused for a long moment, thinking back to her time in Kenya. Meanwhile, Barry squirmed in embarrassment. Finally, she smiled warmly at him. "We're so glad to have you here, Barack."

Barry heaved a sigh of relief when Miss Hefty moved on to the next student, but the day did not get much better. Students continued staring at him. Some of them had never seen a black person their own age before. At recess, a girl came up and wanted to feel his hair, and a boy asked him if his father ate other people. Barry was smart enough to know that the other children weren't trying to be cruel on purpose, but he still felt awkward, like an outsider looking in.

However, in time, the excitement over having a black student whose father was from some funny-sounding African tribe began to die down. Barry then discovered that he neither knew any of the games nor shared any of the same interests that his classmates did. In Indonesia, Barry had played chess, soccer, and badminton. In Hawaii in 1971, kids were riding skateboards and playing football. As Barry tried to catch up, he found that if he could not impress the other students with his football skills, he *could* impress them with exaggerated stories about his father. Of course, Barry had never met his father, and he knew him only through pictures and often-repeated stories. Nonetheless, he found himself telling his classmates that his father was a powerful Kenyan prince and that his grandfather had been the chief of the tribe. What's more, Barry would continue, he himself would one day be a prince in Kenya. Then, in a burst of imagination, Barry announced that *Obama* was Swahili for "burning spear." None of this was true, but it intrigued some of his classmates and made him a few friends.

Then in December, near the end of his first semester at Punahou, something totally unexpected happened. One afternoon, as Barry was in the kitchen making a snack, Toot walked in and leaned on the counter with a letter in her hand. She had an odd expression on her face.

"I have a surprise for you, Barry," she said with a hesitant smile.

Barry looked at the letter in her hand and just nodded.

Toot carefully explained that Barry's mother had always kept in touch with his father. For years, she had let him know how Barry had been doing in school, what his life had been like in Jakarta and Hawaii, and how proud everyone was of him. Toot gently added that Barry's father was also proud of him.

To Barry, this *was* a surprise. He had never imagined that his father knew anything about him—or wanted to. But the surprise was about to get bigger.

Barry's father had been in a terrible car accident not long ago. It had nearly killed him, and he had been in the hospital for a long time.

He still wouldn't be able to return to work for a month, so he had made some other plans in the meantime—he was coming for a visit!

Barry was stunned. He barely knew how to respond to this news. It was very difficult to imagine what it would be like to meet a stranger who was also his father. He knew he should be happy, but he wasn't sure happiness was what he felt.

Then Toot remembered, almost as an afterthought, to tell Barry that his mother would also be coming for a visit during the very same month.

From the other room came Gramps's low laugh. "Should be one hell of a Christmas," he said.

# CHAPTER 3

Many years after Barack Obama met his father for the first time, he wrote about their meeting by saying, "He was much thinner than I had expected. I couldn't imagine him lifting anyone off the ground. If my father hadn't exactly disappointed me, he remained something unknown."

Perhaps young Barry had begun to believe his own imaginative tales about his father being a great warrior and a prince in Kenya. Or maybe, like many boys, he wanted to think of his father as a hero. However, when the big day finally arrived, and Barry walked into Gramps and Toots' living room after school to meet his father, he was surprised by the man who greeted him. Barack Sr. wore thick glasses that made it hard for Barry to see his eyes, he walked with a limp, and he carried a cane.

Barry looked away shyly. Only the day before, Barry's mother had assured him that one day he and his father would be friends. But Barry felt nervous and awkward around this stranger. He even felt guilty for feeling this way; after all, this was his *father*. Barack Sr., however, smiled widely and walked over to put his hand on his son's shoulder.

"Well, Barry, it is a good thing to see you after so long. Very good."

Barry just nodded.

"Your grandmother tells me that you are doing very well in school."

To this, Barry could only offer an embarrassed shrug. As the afternoon and then the evening wore on, Barry watched his father closely but said very little. At the end of the evening, Barack Sr. handed his son a gift of three small wooden figures: a lion, an elephant, and a man in tribal dress. Barry stared at the bits of African art and was not sure what to say.

"They are only small things," Barack Sr. said quietly.

Barry mumbled a "thank you" and went to his room. As he lay in the darkness trying to fall asleep, he wondered if, in fact, he and his father would really ever be good friends.

Gramps, Toot, and Barry's mother were overjoyed to see Barack Sr., but the joy began to wear a bit thin as week after week went by. Barack Sr. began to complain about Barry's study habits which, in his opinion, were not good enough. One night, as the adults sat talking after dinner, Barry was sprawled on the sofa, watching *How the Grinch Stole Christmas.* Suddenly, Barack Sr. turned to Barry and, in a loud voice, said, "You have watched too much television. Go to your room and study now."

What followed was a noisy argument among the adults about whether Barack Sr. had the right to tell Barry when he could or could not watch television. Barack Sr. claimed that Barry was becoming lazy and spoiled and that he would never amount to anything if this continued. Gramps argued right back that Barry had the right to relax during Christmas vacation. In the end, Barry went to his room and slammed his door. He was beginning to resent his father's behaving like a parent—after all, Barack Sr. had never been around for any of Barry's childhood. Soon, Barry was counting the days until his father would return to Kenya. His father was far from being a hero, and he was certainly not a friend.

About a week before Barack Sr. was to leave, Barry received a bit of news that was, in his opinion, just about the worst thing imaginable: Miss Hefty had asked Barack Sr. to speak to Barry's class about Africa and his life in Kenya. Now, all of Barry's classmates would find out that he had lied about his father being a prince. Both he and his father would be the joke of the school.

When the day finally arrived, Barry sat near the back of the room. As his father began talking, Barry stared hard at a corner of the wall, trying to block out what he was certain was going to be complete humiliation. Then, something unexpected happened. Barack Sr. held every student's attention as he spoke passionately about his country, the wild animals and tribes that lived there, and how black people in Kenya, just as in the United States, had been forced into slavery. But just like every one of the students in the room—Barack Sr. looked from student to student as he spoke these words—Kenyans longed to live free. Everyone, he explained, regardless of skin color, must have the right to freedom.

When Barack Sr. was finished, the students applauded for a long time. Later that day, students came up to Barry at recess and lunch to congratulate him on his father's talk.

"Your dad is pretty cool," one boy said. This was the ultimate compliment, particularly since it came from the same boy who had asked, on the first day of school, if Barry's father ate people.

In the days before Barack Sr. left, the distance between Barry and his father seemed to shorten. The two talked, listened to music together, and told jokes. Once, they even danced together to a record of African tribal music, Barack Sr. laughing himself into tears as he limped through the steps. Barry realized that he had been wrong about his father. Perhaps he was a hero after all.

• • •

Fifteen-year-old Barry paced back and forth along the sidelines of the basketball court. Now and then, he'd rush over to the coach and strongly suggest that he put in some second-string players. Barry was not shy about telling the Punahou basketball coach what he thought—particularly when voicing his opinions might mean getting a chance to play. When Barry had started high school at Punahou Academy, he still felt like an outsider at times because of his skin color; but when he played basketball, all the dividing lines seemed to fade away. There was no black or white; there was only the team working together as one to win the game.

Barry would often practice for hours after school. "He was what we called a gym rat," Barry's old coach would later say. "He loved the game so much that he'd do anything to practice. He snuck past teachers when they opened the gym's locked doors. Sometimes he'd even break into the gym." Barry played forward, and his team ultimately won the Hawaii state championship during his senior year. Although he was not the best player on the team, no one tried harder or had more spirit than Barry Obama.

During this time, Ann divorced Lolo and moved back to Hawaii with Barry's half-sister, Maya. Ann, Maya, and Barry all lived together in a small apartment, and money was always tight. To help out, Barry looked after his sister, did the food shopping, and even worked part time at a Baskin-Robbins, scooping ice cream cones. Most of the students at Punahou came from families with a lot of money, and Barry was well aware that some of his classmates looked down on his cheaper clothes or the fact that he lived in an apartment instead of a house.

Barry stayed in touch with his father, sending letters to Kenya and receiving letters in return. Often, his father would talk about the day when Barry would "come home" to Africa and meet his family there. It was difficult for Barry to accept the fact that he had grandparents, aunts, uncles, half-brothers, and half-sisters in Kenya. In his father's letters, Barry mostly searched for any words that might help him understand himself. As a black teenager who had a white mother and white grandparents and went to a practically all-white school, Barry was often confused about his own identity.

• • •

Barry's best friend, Ray, shook his head in anger one afternoon. He and Barry had gone to a party the night before, and none of the girls had given Ray a second look. Ray was one of the few other black students at Punahou, and he always just assumed that the white girls wouldn't date him because they were racist. Barry grinned at his friend and said, "You know, just because a girl won't go out with you doesn't mean she's racist."

But Ray couldn't be convinced. He often lumped all white people together, saying "You know how white folks are" when things didn't go his way or when he felt ignored.

*You know how white folks are.* Barry knew exactly what his friend Ray was talking about. Once, at a tennis match, one of the competitors had told Barry not to touch the schedule because his color might rub off on it. All the other white tennis players had had a good laugh at that. Another time, an older white woman at his grandparents' apartment building had run out of the elevator when Barry had gotten on. She reported him as "following her" when, obviously, he was just using the elevator like anyone else in the building. And just recently, Barry had overheard an assistant basketball coach at Punahou complaining about losing a pick-up game to "a bunch of niggers."

At times like these, Barry couldn't help agreeing with Ray.

Years later, Barack Obama would look back on this confusing time during his teen years and write: "Sometimes I would find myself talking to Ray about *white folks* this or *white folks* that, and I would suddenly remember my mother's smile, and the words that I spoke would seem awkward and false."

Ann had always done her best to teach her son about the civil rights movement, and about Martin Luther King, who had been shot and killed when Barry had been only seven years old. She explained that racism was wrong and that good and intelligent people did not judge others based on skin color. Barry and his mother were close, and these conversations had helped ease some of Barry's confusion when he was younger. However, Barry's mother was not with him for most of his high-school years. In the middle of Barry's sophomore year, she had decided to return to Indonesia for graduate school. She had urged him to come with her, but Barry refused. He didn't want to be the "new kid" yet again at a new school. So, as before, Barry returned to living with Gramps and Toot.

Barry searched for clues to his own identity wherever he could. Gramps had a number of black friends with whom he played cards, drank, or fished, but they didn't have much to say to a teenage kid. Barry listened to the music of black artists and found some comfort in their messages, but no answers. He watched black actors in movies and on television, but mostly he was discouraged by the black characters always being overshadowed by the main characters, who were always white. Barry then turned to books, reading black authors such as Langston Hughes, W.E.B. DuBois, Ralph Ellison, and Malcolm X. Often, he would read late into the night, trying to unravel the mystery of himself. But, as he later wrote, "There was no escape to be had. I kept finding the same anguish, the same doubt."

Finally, Barry decided to look for escape through drinking and smoking marijuana. "I got high to push questions of who I was out of my mind, something that could flatten the landscape of my heart, blur the edges of my memory," he later remembered.

Barry had given up. It was one of the few times in his life that Barack Obama would deny the power of hope.

Except for basketball, Barry began letting everything else slide: his grades, his plans for the future, his self-respect. He stopped writing letters to his father, and he avoided Gramps and Toot. Slowly, his world began to shut down around him as he headed toward what he would later describe as "the final, fatal role of the young would-be black man."

• • •

Ann, having finished her coursework in Indonesia, sat across from her son with a half-worried, half-angry expression on her face. His ambition and his drive to do well at school seemed to have all but disappeared. When she questioned him about it, Barry just patted her hand and assured her that everything was fine.

Perhaps Barry had been able to gloss over his sliding grades and increasing laziness with his grandparents, but Ann would not let him get away with it. She didn't hide her anger as she pointed out that he hadn't even sent off any college applications. She warned him that if he kept going down the same lazy path, he would end up without a career and with no real direction in life.

Barry just shrugged. "Maybe that's what I want out of life. I mean, look at Gramps. He didn't even go to college."

Ann was quiet, and Barry walked to his room. That seemed to be the end of that. But, as they always did, Ann's words sunk deep into Barry's heart. He loved and respected his mother. He knew she was right. It was time for change.

Barry refocused on finishing high school and getting accepted to college, and, as his mother had pointed out, a little effort went a long way. Without trying too hard or really even caring about attending college, he was accepted by Occidental College in Los Angeles.

Before leaving for college, Barry stopped by to see a friend of Gramps's named Frank. Frank was an older black man, a poet, and someone who looked at the world around him with a critical eye. Barry respected Frank's opinions, and he wanted to know what Frank thought about his going to college. Frank looked at Barry for a moment and then simply asked Barry why he wanted to go to college.

Barry thought about this briefly and shrugged. The truth was that he was mostly interested in going to Occidental because he was dating a girl who was also going there. He didn't *really* know why he was headed to Occidental.

"That's the problem, isn't it?" Frank replied. "All you know is that college is the next thing you're supposed to do."

Frank went on to say that he felt that college "trained" black people to forget about what was important to them and to live life according to the rules of white people.

"So what is it you're telling me—that I shouldn't go to college?" Barry asked, confused.

Frank shook his head and sighed. He explained that Barry needed to go to college, but he warned him to be aware of why he was there and what he was learning. "Stay awake," Frank concluded.

So, in the fall of 1979, Barry Obama left for school in Los Angeles. He was, perhaps, no less troubled about his identity as a young man who was the son of a white mother and a black father, but as he watched Honolulu disappear beneath the clouds, he was determined to "stay awake." He would discover all that there was to discover about himself and the world around him.

# CHAPTER 4

"I'm not *black*," Joyce, a young woman with green eyes and African American features, said to Barry. She shook her head as though insulted that Barry had asked her if she would be going to the Black Students' Association meeting on campus. She then told him that her father was Italian, and her mother was part French and part African, and she didn't want to choose between them.

Joyce's reaction was troubling and puzzling to Barry. Throughout his years growing up in Hawaii, he had come to identify himself as black, but here was a woman of mixed race who did not think of herself as black. In fact, she didn't think of herself as any particular race, and she didn't think it was fair that she should have to choose which race she was.

Barry didn't argue with Joyce. Though he wouldn't admit it, part of him agreed with her. Why should someone of mixed race be forced to choose? But a larger part of him fought against the idea of denying his race. *Don't lose yourself*, Frank had said. So Barry made a point of being very careful when choosing his friends at Occidental College. At first, he hung out mostly with other black students, students who were well aware of the struggles that black people had had to endure for many years. These were not students who were about to claim that they were not black. Still, Barry often felt awkward taking part in discussions about the black power and civil rights movements.

One afternoon, Barry was studying at a coffee shop when two of his friends, Marcus and Regina, walked in. Marcus took a look at the book Barry was reading, *Heart of Darkness*, and pulled it out of his hands. In Marcus's opinion, it was a racist book, something Barry shouldn't waste his time reading. But Barry looked at reading the book as a way to better understand how people learn to hate as a result of fear. That, in Barry's opinion, was a very important thing to learn.

After Marcus got his coffee, he headed out, winking at Regina and telling her to set "Barack" straight.

"Marcus is just in one of his preaching moods," Regina said to Barry after Marcus had left. Barry just smiled.

Regina took a sip of coffee. Then she looked puzzled.

"What did Marcus just call you? Some African name?"

"Barack's my given name. It's my father's name. He was Kenyan."

When Regina asked Barry if his name meant something, he told her that it means "Blessed" in Arabic.

"Barack. It's beautiful," Regina said thoughtfully. "Do you mind if I call you Barack?"

"Not as long as you say it right," Barack replied with a grin. And from that point on, Barack no longer introduced himself to anyone as "Barry."

Regina and Barack spent the afternoon talking about their very different childhoods. Barack discovered that Regina had grown up on the South Side of Chicago in a poor, all-black neighborhood. Her father had never been around, but she was constantly surrounded by aunts, uncles, and grandparents, all sitting around the kitchen, laughing and sharing. Barack listened to her talk about her neighbors, the local church, the hard times, and he found himself wishing he had known a life like that, full of the black experience. When he told her that he envied her, she laughed out loud.

"Isn't life something?" she said, still giggling. "And here I was all this time wishing I'd grown up in Hawaii!"

Years later, Barack thought back to that afternoon and wrote, "Strange how a single conversation can change you." Simple as the

conversation may have been, it helped Barack
see that his past was as important and real as
anyone else's. Not only was that afternoon the
point at which he started using his true name; it
was also the point at which he started becoming
his true self.

• • •

Midway through his sophomore year at
Occidental, Barack became involved with
a group of students who were protesting
apartheid in South Africa. "Apartheid" was a
policy that forced blacks to be separated from
whites. It kept blacks from having good jobs
and drove many of them into poverty. It was
quite similar to the "Jim Crow" laws in the
United States—unfair, cruel laws that, in part,
eventually led to the civil rights movement.

Barack and his anti-apartheid friends
decided to hold a rally on one of the college's
big lawns. The rally would begin with Barack
giving a speech about how wrong apartheid was,
but a few minutes into the speech, several of
his friends would storm the stage and drag him
away. The point of this would be to symbolize
how South Africa did not allow blacks to speak
their opinions or have a voice in their own
government.

When the day arrived, Barack was nervous.
He had never given a speech before, and he
wasn't sure if anyone would even listen to him.

He approached the microphone and began in a shaky voice: "There's a struggle going on. It's happening oceans away. But it's a struggle that touches each and every one of us. Whether we know it or not. Whether we want it or not."

Out on the lawn, the Frisbees stopped flying, and the chatter died down. Everyone turned to look at Barack. Then, in a louder, more confident voice, he continued.

"A struggle that demands we choose sides. Not between rich and poor. Not between black and white. It's a choice between fairness and injustice! A choice between right and wrong . . ."

When Barack stopped, the crowd cheered him on, clapping and calling for more. As planned, his friends dragged him off the stage, and Barack pretended to struggle against them so that he could continue his speech. However, Barack found that he wasn't completely pretending. He *wanted* to keep speaking. People had really listened to him. As the rally continued, other people spoke, but the crowd was not nearly as attentive as it had been when Barack had spoken. For the first time, Barack sensed his ability to connect with people. Perhaps, he thought, he could make a difference.

• • •

Near the end of Barack's sophomore year at Occidental, he longed to live "in the heart of a true city." He was weary of Los Angeles with its endless suburbs, perpetual sunny weather, and flashy lifestyle. Barack's first two years of college had changed him. He now had a focus, wanting to finish his degree in political science and work in a career where he could help make the world a better place. Barack had also decided to leave his partying ways behind him, though some of his old party friends at Occidental often tempted him. It was time once again for a change—a big change.

Barack decided to take advantage of Occidental's transfer program, which would allow him to attend Columbia University in New York City for his junior and senior years. In addition to being excited about how different New York would be, Barack was also looking forward to being so close to Harlem. He had never lived in or near a black neighborhood before, and he longed to experience life in this center of black culture and history.

For all his anticipation, Barack's first night in New York City was certainly less than a memorable welcome. Due to a misunderstanding with a friend, Barack found himself banging on the door of an empty apartment at midnight. Without enough money to stay at a hotel, Barack ended up sleeping in the alley behind the apartment and bathing in the water from a fire hydrant in the morning. Luckily, after a few phone calls, Barack was able to contact another friend, who was willing to share his apartment in East Harlem.

"The beauty, the filth, the noise, and the excess, all of it dazzled my senses," Barack wrote of New York City some years later. Still, determined to take better care of himself and do well in school, Barack resisted getting caught up in all the dazzle. He quit drinking completely, began running three miles every day, fasted one day a week, and wrote, as Barack later called it, "very bad poetry" in his journal nearly every night. He worked harder than ever on his studies. Often, the only entertainment he allowed himself was playing basketball at neighborhood courts or going to listen to Reverend Jesse Jackson speak down on 125th Street.

"Man, you're becoming a bore!" Barack's roommate complained one Saturday night after Barack turned down an invitation to a party, once again, in order to study. His roommate pointed out that Barack was not going to change the world with all of his studying.

*Maybe not*, Barack would think, but he was going to try. Sometimes he would take a break and walk from one end of the city to the other, watching people from different backgrounds living their lives. Barack still had questions about his own background and who he really was. Sometimes, seeing the diversity of life around him in the city eased his mind.

However, at other times, his walks troubled him. As he would wander through museums or by high-rise office buildings, he couldn't help noticing that the only black employees were security guards, messengers, or clerks.

Perhaps, like his own father so many years earlier, Barack had his moments of wondering whether he should even try for more than what he saw all around him. Change seemed so impossible. But, like his father, he refused to give up, knowing in his heart that he, too, had the power to make his life different—and better.

●  ●  ●

"Barry's okay, isn't he? I mean, I hope he doesn't become one of those freaks you see on the streets around here." Barack's sister, Maya, was talking in low tones to their mother in the kitchen of Barack's apartment. She and Ann had come to visit Barack the summer before his senior year. He was working at a construction job during the day and continuing to study and read constantly in the evenings. He had bought his sister a stack of novels before her arrival, and he had just scolded her for watching TV instead of reading.

Ann assured her daughter that Barack was fine, though she did worry that her son had gotten too skinny. In more ways than one, Ann thought, Barack was similar to his father.

Later that evening, Barack asked his mother

if she had an international postage stamp. When Ann learned that he and Barack Sr. had been exchanging letters again for the past year, she looked at her son in surprise. Even more surprising was Barack's news that after he graduated the following year, he was planning to visit his father in Kenya. Ann was genuinely pleased to know that Barack was going to visit his father, but she paused and looked at her son for a moment.

"I hope you don't feel resentful towards him," she said quietly.

"Why would I?" Barack asked.

Ann then sat down next to Barack and told him several things she had never told him before. She explained that she, not Barack's father, had asked for the divorce. His father had not left *them*—she had left *him*. Ann went on to point out how complicated their marriage had been. Barack Sr.'s father condemned the marriage, saying that he didn't want a white person's blood in the Obama family tree. Barack Sr. also had another wife in Kenya whom he had married before Ann, and, though he said he had divorced her, he hadn't. Obviously, Ann did not want to be one of several wives, even though polygamy was a Kenyan custom. Still, Ann had never stopped loving Barack Sr.

"We were just so young," Ann finally said with a sigh. "I was younger than you are now."

Barack watched his mother smile and laugh as she told more stories about his father. Later, Barack would write, "She saw my father as everyone hopes at least one other person might see them. And she was trying to make the child who never knew him see him in the same way."

If Barack did not quite see his father as his mother saw him, he at least began seeing things a bit more clearly. Now, he was even more eager to get to know his father. As his mother had hoped many years ago, perhaps he and his father really would become close friends.

• • •

Only a few months after Barack had this conversation with his mother, he received a phone call. The voice on the other end was unfamiliar, a woman's voice with a strong accent. Static crackled through the receiver.

"Barack? Is it you?"

Barack's Aunt Jane, whom he had never met, was calling from Nairobi to give him some very bad news. Barack's father had been in another terrible car accident, and this time he had died. Barack hardly knew what to say to the woman crying on the phone—a stranger, and yet a relative.

Years later, Barack would remember, "I felt no pain, only the vague sense of an opportunity lost." No tears. Nothing. If Barack had been uncertain about how to feel toward his father while he was alive, he was even less sure of how he should feel now that his father was dead. Barack made up his mind to move on and focus on his future. There was nothing else to be done. The past was over.

Almost exactly a year after his father's death, Barack had a dream. In his dream, he was visiting his father in prison. A very thin and painfully sad man, Barack Sr. looked at his son and said, "Barack, I always wanted to tell you how much I love you." Barack tried to joke with his father—anything to make him happier—but his father just looked away and said it would be best if Barack left him alone.

Barack woke from his dream crying, the first tears he'd shed for his father. In the middle of the night, he got up and pulled out all the old letters from his father. As he read through every one, he realized that the past was not over at all. As the first rays of sunlight began to creep over New York City, Barack finished reading the last letter. He now knew that he would continue searching for his father. Even though his father was gone, some day he would come to know him.

## CHAPTER 5

When Barack graduated from Columbia University in the spring of 1983, he summed up his years at that university as "an intense period of study. I spent a lot of time in the library. I didn't socialize that much. I was like a monk."

Even though his years at Columbia had changed Barack, one thing was the same: he still wanted to make the world a better place. To Barack, a lot of changes needed to be made. He saw the Reagan administration as backward, Congress as corrupt, and the people of the United States as rather selfish, concerned more with making money than with helping others. However, Barack knew that progress would have to happen a little at a time; he couldn't change the world overnight.

While his classmates mailed off applications for graduate school, Barack sent off application after application to organizations that helped poor communities. In particular, Barack wanted to help black communities, so he also wrote to civil rights organizations. When his friends asked him what a "community organizer" did, Barack wasn't exactly sure, but he knew that community organizers worked to make the lives of others a little better.

However, when Barack received a grand total of zero responses from all the organizations he had contacted, he decided that he needed to change his plans. It might not be such a bad idea, after all, to work at a 9-to-5 office job for a while to help pay off his student loans. Maybe he could even save a little money for the future. Without much effort, Barack landed a job as a research assistant at a big corporation in Manhattan. Mostly, this work involved collecting information about finances around the world. It was hardly inspiring work for Barack, but he was a good and hardworking employee. Before long, he was promoted and given his own office, with a secretary to answer his calls.

As the only black man at the company, Barack felt a little embarrassed at times. In his opinion, his situation just pointed out how rarely black men were given good jobs. However, there were black women who worked as secretaries, and they were thrilled to see a 22-year-old black man in Barack's position.

"But what I really want to do is community work," Barack would often tell them. "That's my ambition."

The women would shake their heads and ask Barack why in the world he'd want to do a job like that. It didn't pay much, and there certainly wouldn't be a fancy office waiting for him. Even the black security guard, Ike, advised Barack to focus on earning money, rather than helping others. In Ike's opinion, the people Barack would be helping wouldn't even appreciate what he was doing. It would be a waste of Barack's life.

Though Barack found it difficult to explain his reasons for wanting to leave his high-paying, fancy job back then, years later he would sum them up by saying, "There's nothing wrong with making money, but focusing your life solely on making a buck shows a poverty of ambition. We need to steer clear of this poverty of ambition, where people want to drive fancy cars and wear nice clothes and live in nice apartments but don't want to work hard to accomplish these things. Everyone should try to realize their full potential."

● ● ●

One morning, after Barack had been at his job for about six months, a phone call came in from his half-sister, Auma. Auma was the daughter of one of Barack Sr.'s wives, and yet another relative that Barack had never met. She was calling from Kenya, but despite the static, Barack could hear the excitement in her voice.

"I wonder, Barack, if I could come visit you in New York next summer?" she asked.

"Of course, Auma!" Barack responded enthusiastically. As always, he longed to meet his Kenyan relatives. There remained an ache and an emptiness in Barack after his father died that could be eased, he felt, only by meeting his father's side of the family. It haunted him to think that half his family lived half a world away in a culture about which he knew nothing.

As the months leading up to Auma's arrival went by, Barack became less frustrated with his job as he was lulled into the comfort it provided. After all, it paid great money, and his coworkers respected him and treated him well. It was nice to be able to afford an apartment big enough to have friends and family visit. Auma would certainly be impressed, he thought. Maybe this kind of job wasn't so bad after all.

Then Barack was jolted out of his comfortable world. Only weeks before she was supposed to arrive, Auma called in tears; she wouldn't be coming to New York. Her brother, and Barack's half-brother, David, had been killed in a motorcycle accident. When Barack hung up, he was troubled that once again, he had never known a relative who was now gone for good. Who were these people, he wondered, these strangers who shared his blood? Somehow, the death of his half-brother brought what was important in life back into focus for Barack. A nice office, money, a big apartment—none of these things would ever make him truly happy. Acquiring material possessions would never make a difference in the world—or in his life.

Within a month of learning of David's death, Barack quit his job and went back to looking for work as a community organizer.

• • •

Gerald Kellman took a long look at Barack, and then he said, "You must be angry about something."

"What do you mean by that?" Barack said, raising his eyebrows questioningly. He looked at Kellman's face for clues, but didn't see any. Kellman was interviewing Barack for a job as an organizer on the South Side of Chicago, and Barack wanted the job very much.

Running his hand over his beard, Kellman sighed. Then he explained that anger is often a reason for becoming an organizer. After all, if someone isn't fed up with something, he or she wouldn't care about making changes. Barack could see his point. Kellman went on to explain that people on the South Side had lost a lot of jobs because of plant closings and layoffs. The city tended to ignore these poorer people, and they needed someone to help them fight for training centers and job placement programs.

Then Kellman bluntly pointed out that

he also needed someone black to work in the South Side. Often, the people who lived there were suspicious of white community organizers. They were more inclined to trust someone of their own race. Trust, in turn, would lead to the residents working with the organizer to make their neighborhoods better.

At the end of the interview, Kellman offered Barack the job. It would pay $10,000 a year—less than half of what Barack had earned at his old job. He would have to move to a new city where he knew no one. He would be working long hours trying to help people who might not care about what he would be trying to do. Even so, Barack took only moments to make up his mind. "I accepted the job, sight unseen," he later wrote. "I was motivated by a single, simple, powerful idea—that I might play a small part in building a better America."

One week later, Barack left New York City in an old battered Honda Civic that he had bought after accepting the job in Chicago. He had been to Chicago once when he was a child, and his vague memories were of a cold, loud city that frightened him a bit. Now, as he drove through the city, it was beautiful to him, the tall trees lining the lake shore, and the sailboats "like the wings of doves across Lake Michigan." However, there was little time for sightseeing. Kellman wanted Barack to start work right away.

Kellman handed Barack a long list. The list contained names and addresses of some of the people who had been laid off from their jobs. Barack's first job would involve setting up interviews with these people and trying to learn some of their concerns and worries. If he could find a common issue, that would be the first problem he would tackle.

Barack drove through the neighborhoods of the laid-off workers. Many people sat on their front porches, staring idly at the cars going by. Others gathered on street corners to smoke and drink beer. Barack then drove by the shut-down steel plants with their rusted gates, chained doors, and empty lots. He wanted to help these people; but it wouldn't be easy.

More often than not, the people Barack called were reluctant to speak with him. Those who did make appointments often did not show up. Those who did show up usually spent most of the conversation talking about topics that were not real issues: neighbors they didn't like, expensive car repairs, the extremely hot summer. Barack was interviewing people in mostly all-black neighborhoods, and he found, as Kellman had warned him, that some of those he spoke with were not willing to work with people of other races. When they found out that Barack's organization, the

Developing Communities Project, also helped Latinos and white people, they lost interest.

Still, Barack kept talking with the people in these neighborhoods, seeking a common concern. One issue that did come up quite often was the safety of children in some of the poorer, more dangerous communities. Recently, there had been a gang-related shooting that had injured a young person, but the police, who were mostly white, did not seem very interested. The shooting had happened right in front of the home of an elderly woman Barack was interviewing.

"I'll tell you what you ought to do, young man," the woman said to Barack when he mentioned trying to put together a neighborhood meeting to discuss the problem. "You go talk to Reverend Reynolds. He's the pastor of the church right here on this block where the shooting happened. He'll pass the word about the meeting on to his congregation."

Barack was so excited about this idea that he could barely sleep that night. *Finally*, there was something the community could work on together. Perhaps he could even get the district police commander to attend the meeting and hear the neighborhood's concerns. The next morning, Barack called Reverend Reynolds to arrange a meeting with him and several other local ministers to discuss the idea.

Although Barack was nervous about presenting his idea to the group of ministers, he was very convincing. All the older men were quite impressed—except for one.

"What's the name of your organization?" one of the ministers, Reverend Smalls, asked.

"Developing Communities Project," Barack replied.

Reverend Smalls thought about this for a while, and then a sour expression filled his face. He remembered another man coming around a year or so earlier who was also trying to make changes in the community. But this other man was white.

"I told that white man he might as well pack up and get out of here. We don't need nothing like that around here," Reverend Smalls said with disgust.

Barack was too stunned to know what to say. He stammered a few words about the importance of a community working together, but Reverend Smalls waved him off and continued.

"White folks come in here thinking they know what's best for us, hiring a bunch of high-talking college-educated brothers like yourself who don't know no better, and all they want to do is take over."

In the week following the meeting, Barack attempted to follow up with Reverend Reynolds.

After all, *he* had seemed very enthusiastic, and it was his church. However, Reverend Reynolds never returned any of Barack's calls. When Barack talked with Gerald Kellman about what had happened, Kellman laughed. He remembered Reverend Smalls quite well.

"Why didn't you warn me about him, then?" Barack asked angrily.

Kellman just grinned and then gently explained to Barack that it was a good thing that he learned this lesson early on.

On his way home that evening, Barack wondered just exactly what "lesson" he was supposed to have learned. That no race is immune from racism? That there will always be difficult people like Reverend Smalls? That being a community organizer was going to be harder than he had thought? Perhaps the lesson was all that and more. Barack sighed deeply. He knew what he'd have to do next: start all over again.

• • •

The first thing that struck Barack as he drove toward the Altgeld Gardens public housing project was the smell. Before the rows and rows of rundown, identical apartments even appeared, a stink like rotten garbage blew through Barack's open car windows. As he got closer to the projects, he figured out why. To the east of Altgeld was a huge city dump, and to the north was a sewage treatment plant. Between the two were the rows of projects. Peeling paint, muddy lawns, rusty doors hanging on hinges, trash blowing down the pothole-filled streets—Barack took it all in. This neighborhood would be the next area that the Developing Communities Project would try to help. Later, Barack would recall how he felt as he took a look around: "I closed my eyes and leaned my head against the car seat, feeling like the first mate on a sinking ship."

Discouraged as he may have been, Barack did not give up. As before, he went door to door, speaking with the residents and finding out what troubled them the most. Right away, he learned that many apartments had broken pipes, sagging ceilings, and clogged drains and toilets. Worst of all, a poisonous substance, asbestos, had been found in the paint on the walls. This substance was particularly dangerous for small children, who sometimes chewed on the peeling paint. The Chicago Housing Authority was supposed to keep the projects repaired, but they generally ignored requests and complaints from individuals.

With each visit he made, Barack reminded the residents that if they worked together as a group, real change could happen. "It's your community," he would tell them.

At first, few people came to the meetings

Barack organized. Before long, however, word began to spread that a determined young man was trying to pull people together to fight for their rights. In time, more and more parents concerned about the peeling asbestos paint began coming to meetings. Finally, there were enough concerned neighbors to make an impact. Barack filled a bus with the Altgeld residents and drove across town to the Chicago Housing Authority. There, he made his case for how unfairly those who lived at Altgeld had been treated. The residents themselves told personal stories about the terrible conditions at the housing project. In the end, the Chicago Housing Authority agreed to come out and make repairs, strip away the asbestos, and even fill potholes in the community.

As the bus made its way back to Altgeld that evening, an elderly man sitting next to Barack began talking quietly. He told Barack that in the two decades he had been living in the projects, he had seen a lot of changes—all bad ones. Barack had been the first person to come in and really change things for the better. The old man had had his doubts at first about such a young man, but Barack had proven himself.

When Barack thanked him for his kind words, the old man added that it wouldn't be long before all the politicians and important people in Chicago would know Barack's name.

Barack just smiled and looked out the window at the Chicago skyline. Hopefully, when they did know his name, they would pronounce it correctly.

# CHAPTER 6

Gerald Kellman sat talking with Barack. He was warning Barack to be careful about what he said to politicians. Kellman explained that Chicago, with its black and white communities, could be a very divided city. He felt that politicians often used this division to their advantage, telling different groups what they wanted to hear just to get votes.

Barack understood where Kellman was coming from, but surely there must be politicians who wanted to make things better, who weren't looking out for only themselves. When Barack said this to Kellman, Kellman just shrugged. Sometimes he felt that Barack was not realistic about how things really were. Even so, he didn't want to discourage Barack.

"I'll just say this," Kellman continued. "You had better be prepared for that meeting with MET. You got a crowd coming?"

Barack nodded. He *hoped* there would be a crowd. "MET" was the Mayor's Office of Employment and Training, and Barack was meeting with its representatives to discuss setting up some offices near Altgeld Gardens. Although MET had offices all over Chicago, it had continued to pay no attention to the Altgeld area, thereby denying many of the out-of-work people the opportunity to learn new skills and get new jobs. Often, when poorer people were ignored, politics was involved. Some politicians didn't want to spend time and money on groups of people that they felt could give them nothing in return.

If a community organizer like Barack began to annoy certain politicians with demands for fair treatment, they could often find ways to silence him or her. Like it or not, Kellman would often remind Barack, the politicians knew the law. Most of them had been to law school. Barack became increasingly and painfully aware of this fact. Sometimes he wished he had studied law instead of political science.

So, rather than going through political channels, Barack approached MET directly. He pointed out to Cynthia Alvarez, the director of MET, that there were no offices near Altgeld. Then he politely asked if she would come to a community meeting, adding that a hundred or more people from the Altgeld community would be attending. Impressed by how many people in the community were concerned about the issue, Ms. Alvarez agreed to attend the meeting. It would be held at seven o'clock the following Tuesday evening.

At six forty-five on that Tuesday, Barack was beginning to sweat. He had looked at the clock on the wall nearly two dozen times as he constantly paced back and forth. So far, only three people had shown up: a young mother with a crying child, an elderly woman who seemed more interested in the coffee and cookies than in anything else, and a very drunk man who kept falling against the empty chairs. Barack and two of his colleagues, Angela and Shirley, had worked exceedingly hard to put the meeting and presentation together. Now it looked as if it was going to be an embarrassing failure. Then, at two minutes to seven, people began trickling in. By five after seven, crowds were streaming in. And when Ms. Alvarez arrived, there were more than one hundred people present.

The meeting went perfectly, and before it was over, Ms. Alvarez had promised to have a MET center in the Altgeld area within six months. The crowd went wild with applause and cheers. It looked as though the entire evening would go off without a hitch until the drunken man jumped out of his seat and bellowed that he needed a job now. Immediately, Shirley walked over to the man and whispered something in his ear. He gave her a funny look and sat right back down.

When the evening was over, Barack, Shirley, and Angela all hugged. It was the biggest success Barack had yet experienced as a community organizer. He was beginning to feel as though maybe he really *could* do this kind of work.

On the way back to the city, Barack thought about how Shirley had quickly silenced the drunk man. "What did you tell him?" Barack asked.

Shirley, a no-nonsense black woman in her fifties, looked at Barack for a moment and then said with a wink, "You're too young to know."

• • •

"Barack?"

Barack felt a tap on his shoulder and whirled around.

"Auma?"

The two laughed out loud as Barack lifted his sister off the ground in an embrace. Auma had finally arranged for a ten-day visit to Chicago, and as the crowds in O'Hare Airport rushed all around them, the brother and sister who had never met just stood staring at each other with shy smiles. "I knew at that moment," Barack would later write, "somehow, that I loved her, so naturally, so easily and fiercely. Even now I can't explain it; I only know that the love was true, and still is, and I'm grateful for it."

Auma was eager to know all about her brother. "You have to tell me everything," she said as they drove to Barack's apartment. Barack told Auma about growing up in Hawaii, his college years, and his job. He even revealed that he had been in love when he had lived in New York.

"What happened?" Auma asked, noting her brother's sadness when he mentioned the woman.

Barack sighed. The woman was white, he explained, though that didn't seem to make any difference in the relationship at first. Later on, however, they had gotten into a big argument about the reason black people were often angry. The woman had said that anger was just a dead end, while Barack claimed that anger was a way of remembering. In the end, they couldn't agree at all, and everything slowly fell apart.

Auma shook her head and told her brother she was sorry.

"I still have my work," Barack replied.

"Is that enough?" Auma asked.

"Sometimes."

After settling into her room at Barack's apartment, Auma told Barack about her life. She was in Germany in graduate school and dating a German man, and though she wasn't thrilled with the idea of marriage, she wanted a future with this man. After Auma had talked for some time, Barack carefully asked her to tell him about their father. Auma was silent for a long moment. Then she walked over to Barack's bookshelf and picked up a picture of their father.

"I can't say I really knew him, Barack," Auma said. "Maybe nobody did. His life was so scattered. People only knew scraps and pieces, even his own children." Auma stood quietly, still staring at the picture.

Nonetheless, Auma went on to tell Barack what she knew about their father's life. It was a story that both surprised and saddened Barack.

Barack Sr. had returned to Kenya after he finished graduate school at Harvard. After divorcing Ann, he had married another American woman, Ruth, and even though Auma was the child of Barack Sr. and his first wife, whom he had finally divorced, Auma and her brothers were sent to live with their father and Ruth. In Kenya, men had the right to keep the children after a divorce if they wanted them. The mother had no say in the matter. And so, Auma explained, she was then sent to live with a new mother—the first white person she had ever seen.

At first, life had gone well for Barack Sr. He got a good job with the government and was highly-paid and well-respected. However, things were not good in Kenya. Tribes often battled with one another for power or land.

The president of Kenya, Jomo Kenyatta, was from the biggest tribe, while Barack Sr., a Luo, came from the second-largest tribe. Over time, President Kenyatta began to favor his own tribe and mistreat the Luos.

Most of Barack Sr.'s friends kept quiet, but he refused to be silent, Auma explained. He often complained loudly that tribalism was going to ruin Kenya. Word got back to the president, and he fired Barack Sr., saying, "You will not work again until you have no shoes on your feet."

Barack Sr. was trapped. The Kenyan government took away his passport, so he couldn't leave the country to look for work, and no one would hire him in his own country for fear of upsetting the president. Finally, a friend took pity on him and offered him a very low-ranking job at the Water Department. Barack Sr.'s friends all abandoned him, not wanting to be seen with someone the government disliked.

It was a big fall for Barack Sr., and it made him angry and bitter. Before too long, he began drinking heavily; and not long after that, he began losing his temper with Ruth over small things or, sometimes, for no reason at all.

Soon, Ruth had had enough of Barack Sr. She divorced him, taking their son, Mark, with her. Things then went from bad to worse, and Barack Sr. got into a drunk driving accident that had killed the other driver. It had been during this time that he had come to the United States to visit, leaving the children with relatives in Kenya. Barack Sr. had been certain that Ann and Barack would return to Kenya with him and, as Auma described it, "make a proper family." But Ann had turned Barack Sr. down, and when he returned to Kenya, he hit rock bottom. He lost his job at the Water Department, and he and his children became homeless.

"The only thing that saved me was Kenya High School," Auma explained. It had been a boarding school, and when the headmistress found out about Auma's situation, she gave her a scholarship so that she would not have to return to life on the streets. "I just left the Old Man to himself," Auma said, using the family's nickname for her father, "and never looked back."

In time, things got a bit better for Barack Sr. President Kenyatta died, and Barack Sr. was able to get a job again with the government. However, he remained bitter and unhappy. Auma rarely saw him, although just before he died, he came to visit her in Germany. They had a good talk and parted on hopeful terms.

"So do you see, Barack?" Auma finished with tears in her eyes. "I was just starting to know him. When he died, I felt so cheated. As cheated as you must have felt."

Barack was silent. He took the picture from Auma's hands and stared at it.

"You know, the Old Man used to talk about you so much. He was terribly proud of everything you were doing," Auma added gently, putting an arm around her brother's shoulders.

Later that evening, as Auma slept, Barack sat up late thinking about everything his sister had told him. After so many years of hearing what a great and wonderful man his father was, this news had come as an utter shock. All the old stories had been only myths. Some years later, Barack would write: "I felt as if my world had been turned on its head; as if I had woken up to find a blue sun in the yellow sky; or heard animals speaking like men."

Ten days later, Barack took Auma back to the airport. Her visit had been better than Barack could have ever imagined, even if it included learning some difficult truths about his father. As Auma's flight began to board, she grabbed her brother's hand and closed her eyes. It was time for her brother to come to Kenya, she was telling him. It was time for him to come home.

• • •

Gerald Kellman sat at his desk trying to persuade Barack to leave Chicago. Kellman now wanted to focus on Gary, Indiana, a much smaller city, and he wanted Barack to come with him. He tried to convince Barack that Chicago was too big with too many distractions. It was too hard to make any *real* changes.

But Barack shook his head no. He told Kellman that he had just gotten to Chicago. He wasn't ready to leave yet. The fact was, Barack had been working in Chicago for more than two years, but only recently had he felt as if he was beginning to have success.

Kellman agreed that Barack had had some small victories, but he pointed out that small wins are intended to give people courage to fight for bigger things. In Kellman's opinion, Barack was ready for more.

Barack was ready for bigger things, and he agreed with Kellman that it was exceedingly hard to make any big changes in Chicago. Those in power often stood in the way. Still, Barack did not want to move on to a smaller city just because making changes there would be easier. So he stayed behind, continuing to work with Shirley and Angela in other poor communities in and around Chicago, making what small changes they could and hoping that these would give the people in those communities the courage to work for more.

While all this was happening, Barack received a phone call from Auma's brother, and his half-brother, Roy. Roy had moved from

Kenya to Washington, D.C. and wanted Barack to come for a visit. As with Auma, Barack was very excited to meet another relative. But the visit was far from what Barack hoped it would be.

Auma had shown Barack pictures of Roy, a slender and proud young man in African dress, but the man who answered the door looked nothing like the pictures. He was sloppily dressed and very overweight.

"It's the fast food, man," Roy later explained, patting his huge stomach. "It's everywhere! McDonald's. Burger King. You don't even have to get out of the car to get your food."

Roy's memories of the Old Man were mostly bitter and painful. He had nothing good to say about him. In his desperation to escape the pain, Roy had moved to the United States, married, and taken a low-paying job. All of this had been done in a hurry and in an attempt to distance himself from Kenya, from family, from the past. But the past haunted Roy, driving him to drink too much, fight with his wife, and waste his education and intelligence. In Roy, Barack was horrified to realize that he was seeing what his own father had become. The fact that Roy looked just like a fatter version of Barack Sr. only made the parallel more vivid, and it made Barack very sad.

Upon returning to Chicago after visiting Roy, Barack felt a hopelessness that he had trouble shaking. He thought of Roy and his father, two good men brought down by despair. He walked through the neighborhoods of the South Side and considered what Kellman had said: *It's too difficult to make any real changes here.* Barack knew he had two choices. He could either give in to the hopelessness, or he could continue to move forward, making positive changes in his own life.

That next Sunday, Barack decided to attend the South Side's Trinity United Church of Christ. He had heard many of the neighborhood people speak of the inspirational minister and the joyous, exciting services where the congregation sang, shouted, and found the strength to get through another difficult week.

"You must look for that glimmer of hope when everything seems lost!" the minister shouted in a deep voice that Sunday.

"Amen! Preach it!" the congregation shouted right back.

"You know that light is out there!"

"That's right, that's right!"

"You just have to keep looking until you find it. The looking may be hard, brothers and sisters, but there's a bright side somewhere. Don't you rest until you find it!"

"Amen, brother, amen."

Barack would never forget the sermon, titled "The Audacity of Hope," nor would he forget the fiery, magnetic preacher: Reverend Jeremiah Wright.

Barack took the words of the sermon to heart and made two decisions. First, he would apply to Harvard Law School and get his law degree. If those who made all the decisions in Chicago got their power by knowing the law, Barack would learn the law too. But before leaving for law school, Barack would do something that was, perhaps, much more important. He would, as Auma had urged him to do, return to Kenya—the home he had never known.

# CHAPTER 7

Remembering the summer of 1988, Barack wrote: "For three weeks I had traveled alone, down one side of Europe and up the other, by bus and train mostly, a guidebook in my hand. . . . And by the end of the first week or so, I realized that I'd made a mistake. It wasn't that Europe wasn't beautiful; everything was just as I'd imagined it. It just wasn't mine."

Before going to Nairobi, Kenya, to visit his family, Barack took three weeks to travel around Europe and see the places he'd always heard about. However, as he later wrote, he felt out of place and strange in Europe. In the back of his mind, he wondered if he had planned the three weeks in Europe as a way of putting off the trip to Kenya. Friends in Chicago had told him that he would "find himself" in Kenya, that all his questions would be answered.

As he boarded the flight from London to Nairobi, however, Barack wondered whether or not this trip would really answer his questions. He had his doubts, but he was hopeful. On the overnight flight, he sat next to a British student who was on his way to South Africa to work for a year at a high-paying job at a diamond mine.

"Seems like they have a shortage of trained people there," the young man said with a proud smile. Barack carefully responded that he imagined that many of the black South Africans who lived there would be happy to receive training for that kind of work—if only they were given the opportunity.

The British student agreed that that might be true. "The blacks in South Africa aren't starving to death like they do in some of these Godforsaken countries," he said with a shrug. "Best thing to do is mind your own little corner of the world, that's what I say."

Barack held his tongue and stared out the window. If everyone cared only about his or her own little corner of the world, change for the better could never come to, as the British student had called them, these "Godforsaken countries." Barack sighed and closed his eyes. He slept fitfully during the flight, strange dreams and worries waking him several times. Finally, the sun began to rise as the jet descended through the pink clouds. As the world below him slowly came into focus, Barack caught his first glimpse of Africa. He was finally here.

Barack's homecoming was, at first, not quite what he had imagined. His luggage had been lost, and no one was at the airport to pick him up. However, when he asked about his luggage and gave his name, he received an unexpected surprise.

"You wouldn't be related to Dr. Obama, by any chance?" the woman helping him asked. When Barack replied that Dr. Obama was his father, the woman went on to say that her family had been friends with Dr. Obama for years. She shook her head sadly and expressed her sympathy over Barack Sr.'s death. Barack was struck by the fact that someone had recognized his name. Later he would remember, "For the first time in my life, I felt the comfort of identity that a name might provide. No one in Kenya would ask how to spell my name. My name belonged, and so I belonged."

In time, Auma arrived in her old beat-up Volkswagen Beetle. With her was one of Barack's aunts, Zeituni. In the next several days, Barack would meet dozens of relatives. All of them, like Aunt Zeituni, would hug Barack tightly and stare into his face with joy and affection. "You have finally come home!" they would all say. When Auma dropped Zeituni off at her workplace, Zeituni put her hands on her hips and shook her finger at Auma.

"Take care of Barack. Make sure he doesn't get lost again," she said with a serious expression.

As they drove away, Barack asked his sister what his aunt had meant by that. Auma explained that it was a common expression in Kenya. If a family member hasn't been seen in a long time, that person is thought of as being "lost." Even if everyone knows where the family member is, the individual is lost if he or she hasn't been home in a long time.

Barack looked out the car windows at the crowds moving through the dusty streets of Nairobi. Here, he would blend in with the people. No one would judge him on the basis of his skin color. No one would want to touch his hair or demand that he choose sides in a debate about race. Barack turned to his sister and smiled.

He understood completely.

• • •

Life in Nairobi, however, was not without its racial problems. As Auma took Barack around the city the next day, Barack could not help noticing that many of the non-African tourists seemed to act as though they were superior to the natives. At a small restaurant that afternoon, Barack found out why.

"Excuse me! Could we get waited on?" Auma said angrily to the black waiter who had ignored her and Barack ever since they had walked in. In the meantime, however, he had rushed over to a table of white tourists, bowing and smiling and immediately taking their orders. Finally, he reluctantly dropped two menus on Barack and Auma's table, turned his back on them, and continued waiting on the tourists.

"Let's go," Auma said to her brother, shaking her head. On their way out, Auma turned to the waiter and said, "You should be ashamed of yourself." The waiter said something very abruptly to Auma in Swahili. In response, Auma angrily threw a hundred-shilling note (equal to about ten American dollars) on the floor.

"You see! I can pay for my own damn food," she shouted.

Later, when Auma was not so angry, she explained to Barack that all over Kenya, black people treated one another with little respect when it came to money. Most assumed that no one had much money, so the natives were reluctant to wait on one another or provide good service. On the other hand, tourists, because they had money, were treated with the greatest respect and kindness.

Barack tried to soothe his sister's anger by explaining that the same sort of thing happened in poor areas all over the world. However, later he would write: "Not all tourists in Nairobi had come for the wildlife. Some came because Kenya, without shame, offered to re-create an age when the lives of whites in foreign lands rested comfortably on the backs of the darker races."

For several days, Barack continued meeting his African relatives. Everyone commented about how much Barack looked like his father, and everyone had loving and funny stories to tell Barack about the "Old Man." Some of the family, however, were arguing about who should inherit the money that Barack Sr. had left behind when he died. No one had proper paperwork proving a relationship to Barack Sr. None of Barack Sr.'s children could actually prove that he was their father.

In the end, all the bickering was pointless. As Auma explained, there was barely any money to inherit anyway. In Auma's opinion, Barack Sr. had often been too generous. He gave money away to anyone he thought needed it.

Near the end of the week, Barack received a letter from Ruth, the wife who had left Barack Sr. and taken their son, Mark, with her. Ruth still lived in Nairobi, and now she wanted Barack to come by for lunch. Auma shook her head in disgust when Barack told her about the invitation. Ruth had had no contact with the rest of the family for a long time. Auma felt that the only reason she was now asking Barack to visit was so that she could compare him to her son, Mark.

However, Barack felt he should accept the invitation. After all, Mark was his half-brother, too. Also, Barack was curious to meet a young man who, like himself, was the child of a white American woman and their Kenyan father. After arriving at Ruth's home, Barack realized that Auma had been right. Ruth spent most of the lunch making negative comments about Barack's father and trying to put Mark in a better light than Barack. Mark, probably embarrassed, said very little during the lunch. As a result, Barack called Mark a few days later and suggested they meet for dinner, just the two of them.

At that dinner, Barack discovered that he and Mark had very little in common. When Barack explained with some excitement that he had come to Kenya to explore his roots and to learn more about their father, Mark just laughed.

"He was dead to me even when he was still alive. He was a drunk and showed no concern for his wife or children," Mark said matter-of-factly. "Understand—I'm not ashamed of being half Kenyan. I just don't ask myself a lot of questions about what it all means. About who I *really* am."

Later that evening, Barack told Auma about his dinner with Mark. She was quiet for a long minute and then laughed a rather sad laugh. As it turned out, Auma explained, Ruth was the only member of the family who had actually kept all of the documents necessary to prove that Barack Sr. was Mark's father.

In the end, the one person who completely rejected Barack Sr. would inherit the little money he had left behind.

• • •

After Barack had been in Nairobi for about two weeks, he decided that he'd like to go on a safari to see the wild animals of East Africa, and he begged Auma to go along with him. Auma rolled her eyes at the idea.

"How many Kenyans do you think can afford to go on a safari?" she asked. To her, a safari was just another luxury for white tourists, something that native Kenyans would rarely get to enjoy. Still, Barack kept pestering his sister until she finally reluctantly agreed to go.

"But if some animal eats you out there," she said, "I'll never forgive myself."

For the next week, Barack witnessed amazing sights that he would remember all his life. Zebras, giraffes, and wildebeests roamed together through the high grass as the sun rose over an area known as Masai Mara. Lions and cheetahs stalked their prey, suddenly exploding into action. Barack, along with a group, camped out on the wide savannah and saw stars as clear and bright as tiny jewels. The Milky Way was so thick with stars that Barack, at first, thought he was looking at a cloud stretched across the entire length of the sky.

Accompanying the safari group for protection were a few Masai tribesmen dressed in their blood-red robes, carrying spears. These were men from a fierce and ancient tribe. They lived in mud huts and roamed the land with their herds of goats. Barack stared at the Masai, wondering how these quiet, gaunt men could possibly protect anyone from a wild animal. Still, he heard, one evening around the campfire, how young Masai warriors, along with three other young Masai, must prove their manhood by killing a lion together. The only weapons they could use were their thin spears; their only protection, shields made of water buffalo hide.

When Barack commented that it sounded dangerous, the Masai man replied that usually there were only a few scratches. He wasn't bragging, just quietly stating a simple fact. After that, Barack felt safe in the camp.

As the safari continued, Barack became more and more aware of a calm stillness, both in the land spread out before him and in the spirit of those who lived there. More than once, he questioned his "own noisy spirit" that constantly questioned, worried, and wondered. And he thought back to the day his father had spoken to his fifth-grade class. His father had explained that Africa was the place on earth where humankind had first appeared; ultimately, all human beings that would ever live would trace their beginnings back to Africa. Now, Barack looked around him, still evening to hyenas crunched softly on the bones of a killed wildebeest. Later he would write: "This is what Creation looked like. The same stillness, the same crunching of bone. If only we could remember that first common step, that first common word."

• • •

"What does 'Home Squared' mean?" Barack asked Auma. Back from their safari, they were now on a train headed for a small village hundreds of miles away. This was where Barack's grandmother and many Obamas had lived for generations. Traveling with them were several other members of the family, including Roy, who had returned to Kenya from the United States. Roy, Auma, and the others kept referring to their destination as "Home Squared" as though that was the name of the village.

Auma explained that everyone has a home where they live from day to day, but there's also the home in the country where one's ancestors come from—the ancestral home. So, everyone has a home twice over: Home Squared. But, Auma continued, the *real* home is always the one in the country, even if it's only a hut. Even the richest businessman in Nairobi acknowledges that his real home is the hut in the country.

"For you, Barack," Roy said with a grin, "we can call it Home Cubed."

After a day and a half of travel on trains and cramped buses with no seats, the group arrived at a dirt path. They followed the path to a small, low building made of brown mud and surrounded by flowering trees. Chickens pecked at the hard-packed dirt, and two red cows gazed suspiciously at the travelers.

"Home Squared," Auma whispered, a wide smile spreading across her face.

Out of the house walked a large woman in a flowered skirt, wearing a scarf on her head. She grabbed everyone, hugging them as tightly as she could while laughing and chatting in nonstop Swahili. She held Barack's face in her hands and said something excitedly to Auma as she nodded to Barack.

"Granny says she has dreamed about this day, when she would finally meet this son of her son," Auma translated. "She says you've brought her great happiness. She says that now you have finally come home."

Barack learned many things about his ancestors during his time at Home Squared. Granny spoke in a rhythm, going through generations and generations of names, much like the Book of Genesis. She described how the British rule had destroyed the ancient Luo traditions and way of life, and how Barack's grandfather had been one of the first Luo to learn how to speak, read, and write English. Most importantly for Barack, she told him stories about his father's childhood, stories Barack had never heard.

Barack Sr.'s childhood had not been an easy one. Now, Barack learned that his father had been beaten bloody and sent away from home because of his rebellious spirit; that even straight A's had not kept his father from getting expelled from a boarding school after he sneaked into a girls' dormitory; that he was imprisoned as a young man when he became involved in the movement to become free from British rule; that by twenty, his spirit was so beaten down that he almost gave up.

But he had not given up.

After meeting two American teachers who were living in Nairobi, Barack Sr. decided, on their suggestion, to finish a correspondence course and then try to get accepted by an American university. At this point in her story, Granny stood up and brought a box of letters to Barack. The box was packed with copies of dozens of letters that had been sent to colleges and universities all over the United States. Barack held the letters in his hands as tears came to his eyes. His father's letters were just like the dozens he had sent after college when he was looking for a job as a community organizer.

Barack looked at the letters with both pride and sorrow. This was his inheritance.

• • •

Barack knew the rest of the story. His father, even with his Harvard degree, his hard work, and his intelligence, had returned to Kenya, only to be beaten down again. Still, his father had clung desperately to the shreds of hope that remained, believing that there was always a way to a better life. However, the desperation eventually turned to a hard bitterness and pain that would begin to eat away at the Old Man's better nature.

When Auma finished translating Granny's story, Granny led Barack to the back yard. There, on the dusty ground, lay two yellowed tiles. One was engraved "Hussein Onyango Obama, B. 1895. D. 1979." It marked the grave of his grandfather. Next to it, its marker still not engraved after six years, was the grave of his father. Barack brushed his hand across the tile. No longer was his father's life a mystery, blank like the tile. For the first time, his father was a real person to him, and in finally knowing his father, Barack forgave the Old Man his faults.

And in forgiving, Barack fell to his knees on the ground and wept.

# CHAPTER 8

In the fall of 1988, Barack Obama returned from Kenya with a new confidence and a much stronger understanding of himself. Now that his father and his father's family were real to him, Barack finally felt truly prepared to focus on his own future. And he would need that focus—he was entering his first year at Harvard Law School. As Barack walked through the famous campus, he imagined his father, nearly three decades earlier, strolling along the same sidewalks and entering the same buildings. Now, Barack felt a certain pride, knowing that he was, in more ways than one, following in his father's footsteps.

At twenty-seven, Barack was five or six years older than most of the first-year law students. That was not a particularly big age difference, but his classmates often thought of Barack as being even older.

"When you first met him, he seemed older than he was," a former classmate explained. "He seemed experienced in the world in ways some of us weren't. He spoke well and in a way that seemed wise and broad-minded."

Although Barack may not have realized it when he was younger, his travels and his contact with different cultures had benefited him. Because of his recent visits to Europe and Africa and his work with poor people in Chicago, Barack had, indeed, become "broad-minded." He had come to understand that it was a mistake to prejudge others based on first impressions or hearsay. He had experienced firsthand just how important it was for people to work together—even when they didn't agree.

Because he seemed wise beyond his years, Barack's classmates admired him. Even so, sometimes they kept a distance from him, viewing him as someone more like a professor than a fellow student. Barack didn't mind. As at Columbia University, he was usually so busy with studying that he didn't have time for much else. And, certainly, his days of partying were far behind him. Once again, Barack found his main source of entertainment in playing pick-up basketball games around the campus. In 1988, one of the biggest sports stars in the world was NBA basketball player Michael Jordan. Barack looked to Jordan as a symbol of what focus, hard work, and a healthy dose of competitiveness could produce.

While Barack's first year at Harvard Law School was not exactly crammed with social events, he still found time for student activities and interacting with his classmates. As he had done at Occidental, Barack became involved in the university's anti-apartheid movement. At Occidental, apartheid had sounded like a terribly unfair practice. Now, however, Barack had been to Africa and seen for himself just how cruel apartheid could be. As a result, he wrote several moving articles on the subject. One of the articles was published in the *Harvard Civil Rights-Civil Liberties Law Review*. This was a major accomplishment for a first-year student.

Barack also joined the Black Law Students Association. Some people at Harvard were angry that there were so few black professors at the university. Although this was a sensitive subject, Barack was not afraid to speak about it at the association's annual dinner. At the same time, however, Barack argued that a black man or woman should not be hired based simply on the color of his or her skin. If one were *hired* based on skin color, it would be as unfair as being *fired* for the same reason.

Because of Barack's unusual talent for thoughtfully presenting both sides of an issue, both law students and professors quickly learned who he was. People liked Barack because he listened to them—*really* listened. Even if he disagreed with what someone was saying, Barack allowed the person to have his or her say. He was, unlike some of his classmates, in no rush to prove that he was right just for the sake of "winning" an argument. Being right was less important than being fair.

"We need to remind ourselves," Barack would write years later, "despite all our differences, just how much we Americans all share: common hopes, common dreams, a bond that will not break."

Barack's ability to understand this bond, even at a fairly young age, would draw people to him, even people who did not always agree with him.

• • •

"I just don't think it's a good idea for us to go out, Barack. I'm sure you understand why," the attractive black woman said in a low voice, glancing around the office. It was the third time Barack had asked Michelle Robinson out.

"I'm sure I *don't* understand why," Barack said with a little grin.

Michelle sighed. To her, the reasons were obvious. She and Barack worked together. What's more, she was Barack's manager, and managers dating interns was frowned upon.

Barack had moved back to Chicago for the summer following his first year at Harvard Law School. He was working as an intern at a law firm, which meant that he was assigned an attorney to train him and show him the ropes of legal work. Being an intern didn't pay much, but the experience of working for a full summer at a big law firm was extremely important; interns were often the first ones to get good jobs after graduation.

Michelle was the attorney assigned to train Barack. Before Barack even arrived in Chicago, Michelle had formed an opinion about him. There had been a lot of talk in the office about this unusually bright and talented Harvard law student who was coming to intern. Michelle couldn't understand what all the excitement was about. After all, *she* had already graduated with a law degree from Harvard, was working full time as a lawyer, and was two years younger than this supposed hotshot.

"He sounded too good to be true," she told an interviewer years later. "I had dated a lot of brothers who had this kind of reputation coming in, so I figured he was one of these smooth brothers who could talk straight and impress people. So, when we first met he had this bad sport jacket and a cigarette dangling from his mouth, and I thought: 'Oh, here we go. Here's this good-looking, smooth-talking guy. I've been down this road before.'"

Michelle was also a little put off by Barack's unusual name and background. She assumed that a black man raised in Hawaii and Indonesia would be strange and probably stuck-up. Michelle had grown up on Chicago's South Side, not far from where Barack had been a community organizer. Her father had worked in the city water plant, earning just enough money to support the family of four. While Michelle's family was not poor, she certainly had not attended an expensive private academy like Punahou. All in all, Michelle was certain she would dislike Barack Obama.

However, Michelle realized after only a day or two that Barack was nothing like what she had imagined. He was sincere and thoughtful. He was more interested in hearing about Michelle than in talking about himself. When he did talk about himself, he often made jokes or downplayed his achievements. After a few weeks, Barack had asked Michelle to go out with him, but she refused. Aside from the fact that they worked together, they were also the only black employees at the firm. It annoyed Michelle to think that everyone would see them together and think, "Well, of course they're dating. They're both black." Michelle even tried setting Barack up on a date with a friend so that he would stop asking her out, but Barack said no; Michelle was the one he wanted.

Finally, Michelle agreed to go out with Barack for ice cream. After all, that wasn't really a date, was it? But, somehow, a bowl of ice cream turned into hours of conversation. From that point on, though Michelle and Barack remained professional in the office, they began seeing each other more and more.

That summer, Barack returned to doing community work in addition to his internship. One evening, Michelle accompanied Barack when he went to conduct a training seminar for single mothers. He was speaking to the women, telling them they could succeed with their dreams and their plans even if, at times, it seemed impossible. His speech was moving and inspiring, and his concern for the single mothers was genuine. Michelle recalled the end of his speech that evening as being the very moment she fell in love with Barack.

• • •

Back at Harvard Law School, Barack continued to do well. Although his political and social views were fairly liberal, he got along with both liberal and conservative students. For this reason, many of his classmates suggested that he run for the position of president of the *Harvard Law Review*. Being president of this publication was one of the highest honors a law student could achieve.

At first, Barack was not certain he wanted to run. Being president of the *Law Review* would mean having to remain at Harvard over the summer, and he wanted to return to Chicago, both to do summer work and to be with Michelle. In the end, however, friends persuaded him to run. Perhaps more to Barack's surprise than anyone else's, he won. In the 104-year history of the *Harvard Law Review*, no African American had ever been elected president. His election created a media frenzy, and Barack got his first taste of national fame.

In one interview, Barack said, "My being elected shows a lot of progress. But it's important that stories like mine aren't used to say that everything is O.K. for blacks. For every one of me, there are thousands of black students with at least equal talent who don't get a chance." This was the humble, down-to-earth attitude that Barack's colleagues on the *Law Review* admired.

As graduation approached in 1991, law firms all over the United States were trying to persuade Barack to work for them. Some of the most famous firms in the country contacted him, promising huge salaries and luxurious benefits. However, Barack was determined to return to the South Side of Chicago and do the kind of legal work that would help those less fortunate than himself.

One day, a man named Judd Miner, a partner at a firm that worked on civil rights cases in Chicago, decided to see if Barack would be interested in working for him. His firm was not particularly famous, and he couldn't offer the kind of glamour and money that other firms offered. Still, he figured he'd give it a shot and contact Barack.

"Is this a call about a job for Mr. Obama?" the receptionist at the *Law Review* asked.

"Well, yes, I suppose so," Mr. Miner said, surprised that the receptionist would ask that.

"All right, Mr. Miner," the receptionist said with a sigh. "I'll put you on the list of firms that have called. Right now, you're number 647."

Judd Miner was shocked. He knew the competition to hire Barack would be stiff, but not *that* stiff. He hung up, assuming he would never even get a call back from Barack. He was, then, perhaps even more shocked when Barack called back a few days later to politely express his interest in working for Judd Miner. Miner let Barack know that much of the work would involve helping the community on the South Side of Chicago, the exact thing Barack was looking for. He agreed, upon graduation, to come and work for Miner.

In the spring of 1991, Barack graduated from Harvard Law School *magna cum laude*, a Latin phrase meaning "with great honor." Because of his excellent grades and his history-making election as president of the *Harvard Law Review*, a publisher contacted Barack and asked him to write a book about his life. This was quite an honor for a thirty-year-old just out of law school. But the publisher was convinced that Barack's unusual childhood, his struggle with his own identity, and his hard-earned success would add up to a great story. And they did. In time, Barack Obama's *Dreams from My Father* would become a national bestseller.

Barack was eager to return to Chicago. He had come to think of it as his second home, after Hawaii. His connection to the people on the South Side and his ongoing desire to help them made his path clear. Some of his fellow graduates were still not certain where they wanted to work or exactly what kind of law they wanted to focus on, but Barack never doubted his direction.

However, before Barack began working for Judd Miner, he spent six months helping people in Chicago register to vote. The organization he led, "Project Vote," focused on educating black Chicagoans on why voting was important and how to go about getting registered. In the past, the city of Chicago had not paid much attention to how few black people were registered. But now the 1992 presidential election was coming up. The race was between President George Herbert Walker Bush, the Republican incumbent, and Bill Clinton, the Democratic challenger. Many people, including

Barack Obama, felt that a large turnout of black voters could make the difference and lead Clinton to the win.

Barack organized and trained the volunteers. He traveled throughout the black neighborhoods and spoke passionately—not in support of Clinton or against Bush, but simply about the incredible privilege of being able to vote. "It's a Power Thing" became Project Vote's slogan, and, in the end, the knowledge that casting a vote *is* a powerful thing inspired many people. More than 150,000 black people registered to vote in fewer than six months. It was widely agreed that Obama's work to get voters registered did, in fact, make a difference in the national election.

Overlapping with Project Vote were Obama's first days as an attorney with Miner's firm. He was also teaching an evening law class at the University of Chicago and, on weekends, writing his book. All of these commitments meant there was very little time for the other main reason why Obama had been eager to return to Chicago: Michelle Robinson.

"There are times when I want to do everything and be everything," Obama would reflect some years later. "That's always been one of my bigger faults. I mean, there are only so many hours in a day, and that can sometimes get me in trouble."

If he wasn't exactly "in trouble" with Michelle, he wasn't particularly on her good side either. Michelle wanted the two of them to spend more time together. They had continued dating, even while Barack was at Harvard Law School. However, now he was just across town, and sometimes they didn't see each other for days. Making matters worse, Barack tended to enjoy debating with Michelle about whether or not marriage still meant anything. After all, with divorce rates so high, was marriage even worthwhile? Sometimes Barack liked to bring up this topic just to annoy Michelle. He knew that she wanted to marry him. What's more, Barack had always known, almost from the first moment he met Michelle, that she would be the woman he would marry.

One evening, Barack finally took some time off to take Michelle out. He made reservations at one of Chicago's fanciest restaurants. Michelle was enjoying the romantic dinner immensely until Barack brought up the worn-out marriage discussion. Michelle had had enough. She let Barack know that he'd better get serious about their relationship if he wanted it to continue. She was still lecturing Barack when dessert arrived. On her dessert plate was an engagement ring. Michelle stopped talking in mid-sentence.

Years later, Michelle recalled that evening with a laugh: "Barack said, 'That kind of shuts you up, doesn't it?' And, you know, I don't even remember what the dessert was. I don't think I even ate it. I was so shocked and kind of embarrassed because he did sort of shut me up."

The next October, Michelle and Barack were married by Reverend Jeremiah Wright at the United Trinity Church of Christ.

# CHAPTER 9

In 1995, Barack Obama was restless. He had worked a few years as an attorney, focusing mostly on civil rights cases that helped the people of Chicago's South Side. This was work he loved, but sometimes it didn't seem like enough. Barack had become a lawyer so that he would have the expert knowledge needed to bring about change. But now, there were changes that needed to be made that Barack couldn't bring about—unless he became something more than a lawyer.

Barack had never kept his interest in politics a secret from his wife. Michelle, at first, was not too excited about the idea of her husband running for office. She would later explain her feelings this way: "I, like most people, have been very reluctant about politics. Politics is a nasty business, and you don't hold out hope that fairness will win. It's like a business. So, there was that part of me that said 'Do Barack and I want to put ourselves out for a system that I am not sure about?'"

Still, Michelle believed that if anyone could make a difference, Barack could. Perhaps if he were in office, real and good change might come about. So, when he asked for her blessing—something he would always do when he wanted to run for office—she gave him the go-ahead.

Barack had decided to run for the Illinois state senate. The current state senator, Alice Palmer, had decided to leave her position and run for the United States Congress. Palmer believed in Barack and agreed with his views, so she was happy to support him. Then everything changed. When, after campaigning for a few months, Palmer realized that she had no chance of winning the Congressional election, she decided she wanted her old state senate seat back.

Barack said no. His campaigning was going well, and it looked as if he would win. Some people in Illinois were angry at Barack for refusing to step down. They pointed out that he was young and would have many opportunities to run for office, while Palmer, who was much older, would not. However, Barack was both competitive and eager to start his political career. In fact, he was so involved in the campaign that he was not with his mother when she died on November 7, 1995, of ovarian cancer. To this day, Barack claims that not being by his mother's side at that moment is his life's biggest regret.

When Barack was elected to the Illinois senate, he did not get a warm welcome from the other senators. Some thought he was too young and overly ambitious. Others thought he was too proud of his fancy law degree and the fact that he was a published author. Still others were simply jealous; Barack was energetic, positive, and good-looking. Voters from all different backgrounds liked him, a rare achievement that other politicians envied.

In spite of the chilly welcome Barack received, he got to work right away. One of the things that had frustrated Barack in his work as a lawyer was that he couldn't *change* the law; he could only apply it. However, now, as a state senator, he was a lawmaker. He could introduce proposals for laws, known as "bills," and work to get them passed. In Barack's first two terms, he got a total of twenty-eight laws passed. No longer did the other senators question his ability or ambition.

Barack had the unusual ability to present his arguments for new laws in a way that appealed to both Democrats and Republicans. Like Abraham Lincoln, whom he had studied and admired, Barack knew that when people remained divided because of different beliefs, no change for the better could result. Lincoln had once said, "If I do not like a man, I must get to know him better." In the same light, Obama explained, "I think being able to understand both sides of an issue helps me question my own assumptions. It helps me sympathize with people who don't agree with me."

In 1999, Barack and Michelle's first daughter was born. They named her Malia, a word that means "calm" in Hawaiian and "queen" in Swahili. Because of Barack's political career, it seemed only fitting that their first child would be born on the Fourth of July. Barack had accomplished a great deal, but once again he was restless—and perhaps a bit impatient.

"I still burn with the thought of my one loss in politics," Barack would write. "It was a race in which everything that could go wrong did go wrong, in which my own mistakes were compounded by tragedy."

The race Barack would later think back on with regret was against a man named Bobby Rush for a seat in the U.S. House of Representatives. Barack didn't think Rush, an older black politician who had been very involved in the civil rights movement, was a very strong candidate. He thought this would be a perfect opportunity to enter into national politics. However, Barack was wrong.

The district that the winner of this race would represent was mostly black, and, for the first time, voters in that district looked at Barack and questioned if he was "black enough." Rush had been a leader in the black community for years and had lived and served in Chicago for nearly longer than Barack had been alive. Black voters were suspicious of Barack's Hawaiian upbringing, his Harvard law degree, and the fact that his mother's side of the family was white. Still, Barack was in a hurry to move up the ranks and into a position where he could help make even bigger changes.

Two weeks after Barack announced he was going to run, he took a poll. To his alarm, he found out that 90 percent of voters had heard of Bobby Rush, while only 11 percent had heard of Barack Obama. Even worse, Rush's approval rating was at 70 percent, while Barack's was at an embarrassing 8 percent.

"I learned one of the cardinal rules of politics," Barack would later reflect. "Do the poll *before* you announce you're running."

Not long after this, Rush's son was shot and killed by drug dealers. Obviously, after such a tragedy, nobody could say anything negative about Rush. Out of respect, Barack postponed his campaign for two months. During this period, Barack and his family went to Hawaii to visit Gramps and Toot, but on the day they were supposed to return to Chicago, Malia got sick, and they had to delay their trip. As a result, Barack was not in the Illnols senate for an important vote on gun control. Some voters saw this as proof that Barack was spoiled and cared more about a vacation than the lack of gun control—the very problem that had cost Rush his son's life.

"And so, less than halfway into the campaign, I knew in my bones that I was going to lose," Barack would write about that time. He had learned an important and humbling lesson. As in all areas of life, patience is also important in politics. It would take a while, though, for Barack to be able to joke about the fact that he learned this lesson while running against an opponent named "Rush."

• • •

Barack settled back into his work as a state legislator, and in his seven years in this position, he succeeded in getting a variety of laws passed. Focusing on poorer families, Barack helped create laws that provided more money for after-school programs, the removal of lead paint from homes, health care, and AIDS prevention. At times, the Chicago police treated minorities poorly, so Barack worked on passing laws that would cut down on racial profiling, the unfair practice of suspecting a person, on the basis of race or ethnic origin, to have committed a certain crime.

Perhaps Barack's biggest success as a legislator was passing a law that required police officers to be videotaped when they questioned murder suspects. Not long before, in Chicago, thirteen prisoners on death row had been wrongly convicted. Many of them, it became known, had been forced into false confessions during their interrogations. Barack generally opposed the death penalty, but this was not his reason for wanting to videotape questioning of suspects.

"The basic principle is that no innocent person should end up on death row, and no person guilty of murder should go free," Barack explained. He pointed out that film of the interrogations would help both sides—he was not proposing an anti-death penalty bill. In the end, both liberals and conservatives understood the value of such a law, and it passed. During Barack's years in the Illinois senate, he became very well known as a politician who could "reach across the aisle." This meant that, although Republicans and Democrats were separated in the senate chambers (both literally and also politically), Barack was able to connect with both sides. He was a Democrat, but he always considered the Republican viewpoint.

"I make sure that everybody feels they are being listened to," Barack said. "This was something I learned back in the days of community organizing. I learned that it was the way to get things done."

• • •

In 2001, Barack decided to try slowing down just a bit and focusing on home and family for at least a year or so. Because Barack had not been able to raise much money for his campaign against Rush, he and Michelle had used credit cards to help finance part of the campaign. Now they were in debt. So when Barack and Michelle's second daughter, Sasha, was born on June 7, Barack knew it was time to move toward stability.

Then, only a few months later on September 11, 2001, it seemed as though stability could not be further away.

"Now chaos had come to our doorstep," Barack would later write about the terrorist attacks. "Now we would have to act differently, understand the world differently."

Some Americans, however, would choose to understand the world less, to allow their own fear to close their minds. Because the attackers had been of the Muslim faith, some Americans came to believe that *all* Muslims were dangerous and evil. That, of course, could not be further from the truth. Still, there were people who began to point at Barack Obama and question his faith. After all, his name sounded Muslim, and his grandfather (like many Kenyans of that era) had been Muslim. Some went so far as to suggest that Barack was actually covering up his Muslim beliefs by lying and saying he was a Christian. These people believed Barack had a secret, evil plan to harm the United States.

As far-fetched as all these accusations were, they had an effect on how people thought of Barack. For a while, Barack feared that his political career was over. No matter how much good work he had done over the years, it wouldn't mean much if people chose to discriminate against him on the basis of his name and a handful of ridiculous lies.

Luckily, those who knew Barack stood behind him and encouraged him to move forward. In time, he did. He had been lying low, politically, since his loss to Rush—so low that one Chicago reporter jokingly asked, "Is Obama dead?" But in 2002, when a United States senator from Illinois announced that he was going to retire, Obama got the itch to run for higher office again. First, however, he would have to clear this idea with Michelle.

"Before every major decision," Obama once explained with a grin, "I consult two higher powers."

Michelle was not enthusiastic. The family was still in debt, Michelle had a full-time career of her own, and now there were two little girls to raise. She knew all too well that the demands of a campaign would take Barack away from his daughters—and from her. And if he failed in *this* campaign . . . Michelle didn't even want to think about that.

"Look. Here's what's going to happen," Barack promised Michelle. "I'm going to win the primary, win that general election, and then I'm going to write another book to help with the expenses."

Michelle looked at her husband. He seemed so confident, so ready to succeed this time around. He had good reason. His seven years in the state legislature had earned him an excellent reputation. The people of Illinois definitely knew him now, and they liked him—a lot.

"All right," Michelle finally said. Then, covering her smile, she added, "But don't count on my vote."

• • •

Obama was not the only Democrat who wanted that vacant U.S. Senate seat. In the crowd of Democratic hopefuls were politicians who were more experienced, older, and certainly wealthier than Obama. Many political experts assumed that Obama would disappear from the campaign trail rather quickly. They didn't think he could possibly raise enough campaign money to keep going. More importantly, they figured that white working-class voters in the small towns of southern Illinois would not support a young African American candidate. "The typical response to a person of color in these small towns," a magazine reporter bluntly wrote, "is to roll up the car windows."

Obama didn't listen to all the so-called experts. Instead, he followed the same plan that he had always followed when he wanted to get things done: he met the people and listened to *them*. For months, he traveled all over Illinois, meeting people in the cities, towns, and crossroads. He wanted to know what they were concerned about, what troubled them, what gave them hope.

"Barack's got something different," a white factory worker in a small southern Illinois town told reporters. "He makes you feel like he's not a politician, but a leader."

When the primary was finally held, Obama proved all the political experts wrong and won by a fairly large number of votes. Now, all he had to do was defeat the Republican candidate, Alan Keyes, in the general election. Keyes was also a black man, but unlike Obama, he was extremely conservative. Also unlike Obama, he decided to use negative attacks against his opponent. Because Obama supported abortion rights, Keyes questioned whether or not Obama was really a Christian. He suggested, too, that Obama was a sinner for supporting gay rights.

Meanwhile, Obama ran a positive campaign. It was during this time that the campaign slogan, "Yes We Can!" was created. At first, Obama didn't like the slogan, thinking it was too simple. In time, however, he realized that voters wanted an optimistic, direct approach. They wanted to believe that yes, they could be a part of making change. Many politicians had failed to realize one very important fact: Americans want to feel involved in our political system. They don't want to just sit back and watch the politicians make all the decisions. Obama, however, did not fail to realize this.

In the middle of Obama's Senate campaign, the United States entered into war with Iraq. President Bush claimed that Saddam Hussein and his government had weapons of mass destruction even though, it would later be discovered, Bush had no proof whatsoever. The majority of Americans, still reeling and angry because of 9/11, supported the idea of going to war with Iraq. Obama did not. Although he believed that, perhaps, Hussein might be hiding some dangerous weapons, he didn't feel that such action justified going to war with the country.

"What I am opposed to is a dumb war," Obama would say at a rally in Chicago in October, 2002. "What I am opposed to is a rash war, a war based not on reason but on passion, not on principle but on politics."

Opposing the Iraq war was a bold move. Obama, of course, wondered if his view on the war would hurt his chances in the Senate race, but he felt that he had to speak honestly. Keyes wasted no time in using Obama's anti-war sentiments against him, calling him unpatriotic and weak. Still, Obama continued to move forward in a positive way, hoping for the best. Then, in the summer of 2003, an important phone call came in. John Kerry, the Democratic nominee for President of the United States, had a question: Would Obama be interested in presenting the keynote speech at the Democratic National Convention?

The best was about to begin.

# CHAPTER 10

"Tonight is a particular honor for me because, let's face it, my presence on this stage is pretty unlikely."

With these words, Barack Obama began the keynote address at the 2004 Democratic National Convention. The keynote speech at any presidential convention is one of the most important moments of the entire event. The chosen speaker has the responsibility (and honor!) of stating what the party stands for and what it hopes to do for the United States in the next four years. Just before Barack walked on stage in front of thousands of people, television cameras, press, and political experts, he had turned to Michelle and admitted that he was a little nervous. He'd never even used a teleprompter before, and he had certainly never spoken live in front of so many people.

Michelle had given him a hug and, in her typically affectionately teasing way, said, "Just don't screw it up, buddy."

He didn't.

"I stand here today, grateful for the diversity of my heritage, aware that my parents' dreams live on in my two precious daughters," Obama said to a hushed crowd. "I stand here knowing that my story is part of the larger American story, that I owe a debt to all of those who came before me, and that, in no other country on Earth, is my story even possible."

At first, many in the crowd wondered who this tall, thin man with the funny name might be. But as Obama told the story of his unusual background and how, because of the freedoms and the greatness of our country, he was able to make his hopes and dreams come true, the crowd became electrified. Obama was a dynamic and sincere speaker. No one had ever seen a politician quite like him before.

"In the end, that is God's greatest gift to us, the bedrock of this nation; the belief in things not seen; the belief that there are better days ahead. . . . I believe that we have a righteous wind at our backs and that as we stand on the crossroads of history, we can make the right choices, and meet the challenges that face us."

When Obama finished speaking that evening, the entire convention erupted. Many people had tears streaming down their faces, while others could not stop grinning. Writers and reporters rushed to write about this amazing young politician. "I was alone in my den," wrote a *Newsweek* columnist, "looking like a solitary lunatic, but certain that I wasn't alone in standing up and cheering at the TV." Within hours of Obama's speech, many were calling it one of the greatest speeches in recent history. Suddenly, the entire nation knew who Barack Obama was—and now they wanted to know more.

Back in Illinois, the race for the U.S. Senate continued, but after Obama's keynote address, Keyes didn't stand much of a chance. On Election Day, Obama received 70 percent of the vote, winning by a landslide.

Because of the election and his rise to fame after the convention speech, Obama was asked by a publisher to write three books: another memoir and two children's books to be co-written with Michelle. The advance for the three books was $1.9 million. In addition, his *Dreams from My Father* was reissued, bound now for the bestseller list. Not only was Obama able to pay off his credit cards and student loans; he also paid cash for a beautiful new home for his family.

As Michelle and Barack flew to Washington, D.C. in January, 2005 for Barack's swearing in as the freshman senator from Illinois, Michelle remembered the promises her husband had made before beginning the Senate race.

"I can't believe you pulled it off," she said, with a smile and a kiss on his cheek.

• • •

"Daddy, are you going to be president?" six-year-old Malia innocently asked her father when he was sworn in as a United States senator in January, 2005. Obama just smiled at his daughter. Advisers close to Obama were already quietly urging the new senator to consider a run for the presidency in 2008. Obama, they said, was a true symbol of the hope and change our country needed. They pointed out that the outgoing president, George W. Bush, a Republican, had become a very unpopular president. It was time for a Democrat to take the office. The entire country now knew who Obama was. It was his time.

However, Obama wanted to focus on the task at hand first. He didn't want the other senators to think he was too ambitious. After all, in terms of seniority—the length of time served in the Senate—Obama ranked 99th out of 100 senators, only one spot away from the bottom. Also, Obama was the only African American United States senator. He was, in fact, only the fifth black person to have *ever* been elected to the Senate. He wanted to prove himself as a good senator before considering any next steps.

After much discussion, Michelle and Barack

decided it would be best for Michelle, Malia, and Sasha to stay in Chicago instead of moving to Washington, D.C. Many families of senators had made similar decisions. So Barack rented an apartment in Washington and stayed there Monday through Thursday, flying home on Friday afternoons. Sometimes it was lonely for Barack, and he missed his two young daughters terribly, often regretting that he wasn't there to see them every evening. Still, it gave Barack the time and focus he needed to learn the ropes of being a senator.

"It's like trying to drink from a fire hose," Obama later wrote about the experience of being a new United States senator. There were so many things to learn, so many people asking for his time, so many demands, that Obama had to be careful not to become overwhelmed. And, unlike other new senators, Obama also had the extra pressure of living up to his ever-growing fame. Some claimed that he was approaching rock-star status, and magazines, newspapers, and the paparazzi chased him down for interviews and pictures. Many supporters were becoming eager to hear Obama say that he would consider running for president.

Meanwhile, Obama was developing his vision for what he wanted to accomplish as a senator.

"Where I can probably make a unique contribution is in helping to bring people together and to show them how we're all joined together—black and white, rich and poor, even conservative and liberal," Obama explained to a reporter. As always, Obama felt that the very lack of progress or change that people complained about was a direct result of people often refusing to see both sides of an issue and work together.

In his first year in the Senate, Obama did not always vote for an issue just because Democrats or liberals supported it; he voted for what he felt was right. Democrats were upset when Obama sided with Republicans to limit the amount of money that a group of people could sue for when a corporation had harmed them in some way (known as a "class action lawsuit"). But Obama explained that when people were concerned more about winning money in a lawsuit than about changing the harmful behaviors of a big company, then nobody really won. In the end, many Democrats agreed with him.

Republicans continued to dislike Obama's opposition to the Iraq War. He maintained that the United States had gone to war irresponsibly and that we should not continue spending money and lives on a war that had been entered into for flimsy, even nonexistent reasons. "I don't oppose war in all circumstances," Obama explained. "I oppose a dumb war." His words angered many conservatives who, as Keyes had done, accused him of being unpatriotic. In time, however, many Republicans would share Obama's views—views that had not been popular with either Republicans *or* Democrats when he had first voiced them at the start of the Iraq War.

• • •

"George Bush doesn't care about black people," singer Kanye West said with disgust to a live national audience. He was appearing in a televised concert to raise money for the victims of Hurricane Katrina, and he said bluntly what some people thought privately. Following the hurricane, many people felt that the Federal Government dragged its feet in responding to the disaster. Some, like Kanye West, believed that the president didn't act quickly simply because the people affected were poor and black. Others suggested that if the same kind of disaster had hit a rich white area, the government would have rushed to help the victims.

Because of West's comments and the growing anger among many African Americans, all eyes turned to Barack Obama. What did *he* think? Certainly, as a black man, Obama must be angry too. Obama, in a televised interview, placed the blame on both Republicans and

Democrats. He pointed out that the current administration was out of touch and could not even imagine the kind of poverty that existed in the Ninth Ward of New Orleans: "The administration is so detached from the inner-city life in New Orleans that they couldn't imagine that the people there couldn't load up their SUVs and drive off to a hotel with a credit card." As a result, it didn't occur to the president or to those in the Department of Homeland Security that many people were literally too poor to escape the flooding.

On the other hand, Obama did not let Democrats off the hook either. He said that Democrats were also guilty of not understanding just how big the problem of poverty was in the United States. All in all, Obama refused to agree with the idea that people in the Ninth Ward were neglected because of their skin color. "The incompetence of the administration was color-blind," Obama summed up. Essentially, the slow response to the disaster had been a result of ignorance, not racism.

• • •

By mid-2006, Obama's feelings about a run for the presidency were beginning to change. He had gained a good bit of confidence during his first year and a half in the Senate. He had quickly built a reputation as a senator who could bring Republicans and Democrats together, something that was desperately needed in the United States

"Look, if Barack disagrees with you," said one of the most conservative Republican senators in Congress, "he's the kind of guy who will talk to you about it. He'll come right up to you and reconcile."

"Obama is a walking, talking hope machine," said another conservative, who had worked as an aide to George W. Bush. "People see him as a reflection of what is good and great about America. He's like a mirror of what people think we ought to be."

If Republicans were willing to admit that Obama had mass appeal and would be a strong opponent in a presidential race, Democrats were becoming more and more eager to hear Obama say he was going to run for president. Still, there were those who suggested that perhaps he should wait until 2012 to run; that after six or seven years in the Senate, he'd be more prepared.

"I don't want to wait until he's ready!" responded one Washington Democratic insider. "I'm ready for Barack Obama *now*. I don't think we have six years to wait for him, because things are going to hell in a hand basket."

Although Obama had not publicly announced any interest in running, he had been following the advice of some of his political advisers, who had suggested he become even more familiar with what American people wanted, feared, and hoped for. As a result, Obama held nearly forty "town hall" meetings all across Illinois, listening to the people he represented. If he were going to consider the highest office in the nation, he didn't want to make the mistake of being out of touch with its citizens.

"I answer to the people who sent me to Washington," Obama explained. "They ask me about prescription drugs, the deficit, human rights, bird flu, school funding. . . . And as I look out over the crowds, I somehow feel encouraged. My time with them is like a dip in a cool stream. I feel cleansed afterward, glad for the work I have chosen."

In addition to learning more about the people of his own country during his first two years in the Senate, Barack also traveled around the world. He knew that some people might criticize his lack of international experience if he decided to run for president. So he traveled to Russia, the Middle East, and Iraq as a member of the Foreign Relations Committee.

Finally, Obama knew there was one more thing he had to do before making up his mind about whether or not to enter the 2008 presidential race: he must return to Kenya. This time, he took his family with him.

"This trip has symbolic power," Obama told the press. "It allows me to really target a wide range of issues that come up on the international stage and help Americans appreciate how much our fates are linked with the African continent."

Obama's second trip to Kenya was quite a bit different from his first visit many years earlier. Kenyans gathered in huge crowds, trailing the reporters who followed Obama and his family. Everyone wanted a glimpse of this native son who was now a famous United States senator. To Kenyans, he was their own hero, who had come home for a visit.

"This is where he belongs," said a beaming Kenyan woman in a crowd in Nairobi. "He just goes to the United States to work, but he should and will come back home to be one of our own some day."

Michelle and the two girls got to meet Barack's Kenyan relatives. Granny at "Home Squared" was the most excited to see her grandson and his family. While she was proud of Obama's achievements, his fame meant less to her than his return to his ancestral home. And when reporters asked Obama if Granny had given him any advice, he grinned and said, "She told me that I shouldn't trust reporters."

Before leaving Africa, Obama met with Bishop Desmond Tutu in South Africa.

Tutu had been an outspoken activist against apartheid in the 1980s, and he had spent his life fighting against racism, poverty, and AIDS in Africa. Winner of the 1984 Nobel Peace Prize, Tutu was someone Obama had always admired. It was a tremendous honor to meet him.

As the press hovered around, Tutu winked at Obama and said, "You are going to be a very credible presidential candidate."

Obama looked uncomfortable. The entire time he had been in Africa, no one had mentioned the possibility of his running for president. "Oh no, don't do that," Obama replied jokingly.

Tutu laughed and turned to the press. "Fortunately, because he has my complexion, we can't see that he is blushing."

Immediately, the press wanted to know why Tutu thought Obama might make a good president. Tutu answered simply, "People are looking for leaders of whom they can be proud."

• • •

"I believe that we cannot solve the challenges of our time unless we solve them together. And that is why, in the shadow of the Old State Capitol, where Lincoln once called on a divided house to stand together, where common hopes and common dreams still live, I stand before you today to announce my candidacy for president of the United States."

In February, 2007, on a bitterly cold day, Barack Obama made this announcement on the steps of the Illinois capitol building. Thousands braved the single-digit temperatures to cheer him on, chanting "Obama! Obama!" over and over. Obama had once again returned from Africa with the confidence he needed for a task ahead. However, as with all his campaigns, he had first discussed this, the ultimate campaign, with Michelle. Michelle had her doubts about a run for the presidency, but, ultimately, she would tell *USA Today*, "I never had any doubt about what Barack could offer, and that's what kind of spiraled me out of my own doubt. I don't want to be the person that holds back a potential answer to the nation's challenges."

Still, Michelle asked her husband to make a promise before she gave her blessing. "I asked him to quit smoking. For good," Michelle revealed to the press. Obama had tried kicking the habit for years, but now he threw out his cigarettes and gave Michelle the promise she wanted to hear. In return, she gave him the go-ahead.

Barack Obama would not wait another four years. It was time.

"We should take heart, because we've changed this country before. . . . Each and every time, a new generation has risen up and done what's needed to be done," Obama said confidently on that cold February day. "Today we are called once more—and it is time for our generation to answer that call."

• • •

The evening after Obama announced his candidacy, he sat down with his daughters to try to explain what would be happening over the next year or more. Finally answering her question of two years earlier, Obama told Malia that, yes, he was going to at least *try* to become president.

Malia, however, was two years older now—and two years wiser. "So, you're going to try to be president?" Malia asked, unimpressed. "Shouldn't you be vice president first?"

# CHAPTER 11

"**I**'m a fan of his, but whites will never elect him president. When it's time to go into the voting booth, they're not going to pull that lever," a *Chicago Sun-Times* reporter wrote.

"Obamamaniacs must be smoking something," joked a *New York* magazine columnist. "For all his promise, Obama is basically an empty vessel."

"Thirty-four percent of Americans have no idea who this Obama even is," a poll revealed six months after Obama entered the race.

Almost immediately after Obama announced that he would be entering the presidential race, the political experts and the poll-takers began predicting that he would not stand a chance. Some felt he was just not experienced enough. Others claimed he was too unknown. Still others shook their heads, believing that America was not yet ready to elect an African American president.

Obama took it all in stride. "I think there's the possibility—not the certainty, but the possibility—that not only can I win this election, but that I can also transform the country in the process," he said to the doubters. Obama's plan was to run a different kind of campaign, one that would bring people together, not further divide them. He had been in politics long enough to see his share of negative campaigns. Name-calling, bitter attacks, and desperate attempts to get support by focusing on divisive issues were all too common. But Obama had another approach.

"I know Americans are looking for something new and different in politics," he told a crowd in Iowa. "The bitter politics of the past can change if everyone works together. I want to unite America. I want to work closely with people who disagree with me so that we might find common ground."

In fact, Obama had always believed that the United States was not defined by the conservative "Red States" and the more liberal "Blue States" that showed up on political maps. That sort of stereotyping, he felt, only hurt us.

"We worship an awesome God in the Blue States, and we don't like federal agents poking around our libraries in the Red States. We coach Little League in the Blue States and, yes, we have gay friends in the Red States," Obama said, making the point that in the end, we are

one country—the *United* States—and not so
divided after all.

• • •

In a short time, the list of those who
wanted to be the next Democratic nominee
for president got longer and longer. When the
number of candidates reached eight, far more
than usual, Obama commented, "I'd say we're
gonna have some silly season goin' on!"

Although he joked about the length of the
list, Obama knew that some of the names on
that list were no laughing matter. Obama's
biggest competition would come from Hillary
Clinton and John Edwards. Both were experienced senators. Clinton, of course, had already
lived in the White House for eight years as the
First Lady. And Edwards had been John Kerry's
pick for vice president in 2004. Most people
assumed that the frontrunners would be Edwards and Clinton, with Obama possibly coming in a distant third.

However, whoever wanted to move up
quickly on the list would need to win the Iowa
caucus. This was the first of the primaries, the
individual state races that choose candidates for
the November election. The winner would be
the focus of the press and a candidate everyone
would take seriously. Although the Iowa caucus
would not take place until January 3, 2008,
Obama wasted no time. Immediately following

his announcement in February, 2007, Obama boarded a jet to Iowa. It was time to meet the people.

•  •  •

"For me, in my lifetime," a white woman from Texas told a reporter from the *Washington Post* the day after Obama's announcement, "it is truly possible that an African American man can be the president of the United States. My family, my mother, my aunts and uncles might get to see that in their lifetime. It makes me almost want to cry just thinking about it."

In a blue-collar Chicago bar, a burly construction worker heard that Obama was already headed to Iowa. "Our nation needs this guy," he said sincerely. "I'll walk to Iowa, if I have to, to help this man."

In South Carolina, a teacher who had heard Obama more than once said, "He speaks of things that touch the heart of everyday people."

Truly, it would be these "everyday people" who would become the heart and soul of Obama's campaign—in more ways than one.

Perhaps the most difficult job for any candidate is fundraising. If the candidate is not connected to rich people or businesses that might make large donations, this job is even harder. Typically, candidates received the smallest portion of their fundraising from thousands of little donations from ordinary supporters; the largest part would come from a handful of very wealthy individuals. Many millions of dollars would be needed to run a successful campaign.

Both Edwards and Clinton raised their campaign finances the old way. They had some very rich supporters, so the small donations from the "everyday people" across the United States were not quite as important. They would get the bulk of the money they'd need to run their campaigns from people they knew personally.

Obama, however, wanted to try something new.

"No campaign is better at using new technology than Obama's," *Time* magazine reported, several months into the race. Unlike the other candidates, Obama and his advisers had a clear idea of just how powerful the Internet could be in both fundraising and attracting younger voters. They were well aware of the fact that these younger voters no longer watched the news on TV or read newspapers—they went immediately to the Internet to catch up on daily events. Through his own website (barackobama.com) and a presence on *Facebook*, *LinkedIn*, and *MySpace*, Obama was suddenly, with just a few keystrokes, accessible to millions of people. Voters could see replays of

Obama's ads and speeches, join social networks to talk about him, find out where he would be speaking next, and even watch the video "Yes We Can" by hip-hop artist will.i.am.

However, people did more than just visit Obama's website to learn more about him. While they were there, they donated money directly to his campaign. A running tally of "People donating to our campaign for change" blazed across the top of the home page. By March 2007, 100,000 people had given money online, most of them donating small amounts. By June 2007, 250,000 people had given money to Obama's campaign through his website, helping bring the total to $58 million in just six months of fundraising. And by the end of the campaign, Obama's website had received three million donations of $200 or less. No presidential candidate had ever raised so much money through small individual donations.

"Our movement," said Obama's campaign manager, "is both bigger and deeper than anything presidential politics has ever seen." Both the Clinton and Edwards campaigns had underestimated the power of the "everyday person." In six months, the Obama campaign had raised an astounding $58 million, more than any of his competitors. At the same time, the nation was growing more and more interested in this young, different politician.

Clinton and Edwards tried to use Obama's youth as a negative. They claimed he was inexperienced and didn't know the ways of Washington well enough to be president.

"I may not have spent a lot of time learning the ways of Washington," Obama responded at many of his rallies, "but I've been there long enough to know that the ways of Washington have to change."

People loved this new approach. Obama was quickly gaining ground, but would he gain enough ground to win Iowa? Knowing just how critical winning this first primary was, Michelle Obama bluntly told the press, "If Barack doesn't win Iowa, it is all just a dream."

• • •

"You have to fight back. You need to punch harder," worried campaign staffers advised Obama after his first debate with the other Democratic hopefuls in the summer of 2007. Front-runner Hillary Clinton had not held back when attacking Obama during the televised event.

"But that's not who I am," Obama explained with a shrug. "I'm not interested in tearing into Hillary Clinton. I think she is an admirable person and a good senator." Obama did not want to run an angry or mean campaign. He intended to run his race as "the politics of hope," not politics as usual. But those who had followed presidential campaigns for decades knew that opponents could get crushed if they did not defend themselves against attacks. "You must at least engage," Obama's campaign manager told him.

As the summer wore on and the debates continued, Obama refrained from attacking his opponents, but he did begin to defend himself against Clinton's accusations. One of Clinton's main arguments for why Obama should not be president was that he was not experienced in foreign policy. However, Clinton had voted in favor of going to war in Iraq, while Obama had opposed the war from the beginning. "I continue to believe that on the biggest foreign policy disaster of a generation, she got it wrong and I got it right," Obama told *Time* magazine. By mid-2007, more and more Americans were agreeing with Obama.

However, despite Obama's swelling popularity, his groundbreaking fundraising, and his stance on the war, most political experts predicted that he would come in third behind Clinton and Edwards in Iowa. Even when new polls revealed that only one in twenty voters said they would not vote for a black candidate, it was assumed that white voters, in general, would not cast their votes for Obama. And Iowa was a very white state. Many thought that Obama might drop out of the race completely after Iowa.

But they were wrong.

◆ ◆ ◆

"They said this day would never come!" Obama spoke to a big crowd in Iowa on January 3, 2008. "This is a defining moment in American history."

Barack Obama, much to everyone's surprise, had just won the Iowa caucus. The *Washington Post* claimed that his unexpected victory in an overwhelmingly white state "showed us the America we like to believe we live in. It was one of those moments that give you goose bumps." As the Iowa results were analyzed, another surprising fact was revealed: Obama's win was due mostly to voters under the age of 25. Suddenly, young voters were inspired in a way they'd never been before.

"There seems to be a youthquake," a *Time* magazine writer observed. "Young people sense that they are coming of age at a time when leadership, and their role in choosing it, *really* matters."

But the excitement over Obama's victory was short-lived. The New Hampshire primary followed the Iowa caucus, and this time Hillary Clinton won. Obama, having learned his lesson about being too optimistic and impatient in politics years ago, took it in stride. Winning Iowa had been huge, but it was no guarantee. At the same time, he refused to listen to those who claimed that Iowa had been a fluke, an odd twist of luck.

For the next two months, the victories would go back and forth—first Obama would win a primary, and then Clinton would win one. Most of the other candidates, including John Edwards, began dropping out of the race, realizing that the battle for the Democratic presidential nomination had come down to two: Obama and Clinton.

Regardless of whether Obama or Clinton won, history would be made; for the first time ever, the Democrats' choice for president would be either a woman or an African American.

• • •

In mid-March, 2008, Obama's race seemed to be picking up steam. This was fortunate, since the Pennsylvania primary, an extremely important primary, was only weeks away. Many believed that whoever won Pennsylvania would finally win the nomination. It was very important for everything to go just right for Obama for the next several weeks.

Then, a bombshell hit. A tape of a sermon that Reverend Jeremiah Wright had given shortly after the 9/11 terrorist attacks made its way to the media.

"Racism is how this country was founded and how this country is still run!" bellowed an angry Reverend Wright. "The United States believes in white supremacy and black inferiority and believes it more than we believe in God. . . . But white America got a wake-up call after 9/11. . . . God damn America!"

Reverend Wright's furious sermon, which basically blamed white Americans for the 9/11 attacks, stunned people, both white and black, across the United States. Excerpts from the sermon were played constantly on news programs and on the Internet. Immediately, some people began questioning Obama's views on race. After all, through the years, Obama had remained very close to Reverend Wright. He had performed Michelle and Barack's wedding ceremony. He had even baptized the Obamas' daughters. If Obama's closest spiritual adviser had these ideas, didn't Obama, too?

Obama's campaign manager urged him to speak out against Wright, but, at first, Obama was reluctant. Just as Hillary Clinton did not want gender to be an issue in her campaign, neither did Obama want race to be an issue in his. So far, on the campaign trail, he had brushed off race-related comments. Bill Clinton had unfairly suggested that the reason Obama had won the South Carolina primary was that there were so many black voters in that state. Geraldine Ferraro, the first woman to be chosen, in 1984, as a vice-presidential running mate, stated that Obama was "lucky" to be black. She felt that he would not be in the position he was in if he were white.

Obama had not responded negatively to these comments even though the press had pushed him to fight back. Now, however, Reverend Wright's angry words and Obama's connection to Wright threatened to destroy Obama's campaign. He *had* to say something. So Obama spent three nights in a row working very hard on a speech. He was a good speech-writer, but this particular speech would not be easy.

Finally, Obama was ready. He delivered a half-hour address at the National Constitution Center in Philadelphia. Its title was "A More Perfect Union," and it was a moving, personal speech about our country's racial struggles. In it, Obama made it clear that he did not agree with Reverend Wright's sermon. Still, he defended Wright's anger, a bitterness built up from years of oppression and unfair treatment.

"I can no more disown him than I can disown the black community," Obama said of Wright. "I can no more disown him than I can my white grandmother—a woman who helped raise me, a woman who sacrificed again and again for me, a woman who loves me as much as she loves anything in this world, but a woman who once confessed her fear of black men who passed by her on the street, and who on more than one occasion has uttered racial or ethnic stereotypes that made me cringe.

"These people are a part of me. And they are a part of America, this country that I love."

As always, Obama showed his ability to empathize with both sides. He understood why some African Americans were angry with white Americans. Yet he also understood why some white Americans resented or feared blacks. Echoing the words of the Constitution, Obama asked that Americans try to understand one another, to make better attempts at healing racial wounds, in an effort to form "a more perfect union."

When Obama finished and walked backstage, his entire staff, his friends, and his wife were all in tears. Rarely had they ever been so moved by a speech.

"This whole Reverend Wright mess has been a blessing in disguise!" an emotional friend said to Obama. Obama shook his head. It was hard to think of what had happened as a good thing.

Blessing or not, in the days that followed, his heartfelt and thoughtful words were being hailed as one of the best speeches of a generation. Many compared "A More Perfect Union" to another landmark speech on race: Dr. Martin Luther King's "I Have a Dream."

● ● ●

"The Democrats are destroying themselves!" a Republican political analyst gleefully told *New York* magazine.

With only weeks left in the primary season, Obama had pulled far enough ahead of Clinton that many felt she should drop out of the race. After all, the sooner Obama could be the official Democratic nominee, the sooner he and his party could get to work. The Republicans, weeks earlier, had chosen John McCain as their candidate. While the Democrats still were fighting each other in primaries, the Republicans were already working on their strategies for the presidential election.

Some Democrats were irritated with Clinton and wanted Obama to confront her and ask her to give up her campaign. Obama said no. If Hillary Clinton wanted to stay in the race until the very end, Obama said, that was her right. "No Drama Obama," as some had started calling him, would remain true to his word. He would not engage in fighting or ridiculing his opponent.

Finally, on June 3, 2008, Obama had won enough states to be named the official nominee of the Democratic party. Nationwide, headlines shouted the news. History was happening right before our eyes. For the first time ever, an African American had been nominated by a major party to run for president of the United States.

However, Obama took only a moment to enjoy this achievement. His mind was already racing ahead. There were barely five months left until Election Day.

Now the real work was about to begin.

# CHAPTER 12

"If we continue to do the same things over and over again, I believe we get the same results. When you listen to Barack Obama, when you really hear him, you witness a very rare thing. You witness a politician who has an ear for eloquence and a tongue dipped in the unvarnished truth. . . . For the very first time in my life, I feel compelled to stand up and to speak out for the man who I believe has a new vision for America. I am here to tell you, Iowa, he is the one. He is the one!"

Oprah Winfrey was speaking to a cheering crowd in Iowa as she introduced Obama in late June of 2008. The race between Barack Obama and John McCain was now in full swing. Obama was determined to continue his campaign in the same "no drama" fashion he had followed throughout the primary season. Some people thought his cool, calm style would hurt him in the polls, that it would be mistaken for indifference or snobbery. Besides, running negative, name-calling campaigns had been what presidential candidates had done since the days of Thomas Jefferson! Why change now?

*Vote for Change.*

*Change We Can Believe In.*

*Our Time for Change.*

*It's about Time. It's about Change.*

Obama's campaign slogans said it all. It was not going to be politics as usual this time around. Obama had promised voters a different kind of campaign from the very beginning, and he wasn't about to go back on his word now.

The McCain camp, however, did not feel the same way. Right away, some of McCain's closest advisers began mocking Obama by calling him "The One," a reference to Oprah's introduction. They felt the media, like Oprah, was too adoring of Obama and that, as a result, the press was virtually ignoring McCain. This unequal treatment made them angry.

"He's all show and no substance," scoffed one McCain staffer about Obama. "People treat him like he's a rock star or something."

Truly, wherever Obama travelled, tremendous crowds came to hear him speak. They chanted his name, screamed when he came on stage, and pushed and shoved to get a chance to shake his hand or simply get close to him. Obama's speeches were a combination of inspiration, humor, and down-to-earth honesty. Reporters often described the crowds as being "mesmerized" by Obama's natural ability to connect with them.

John McCain, on the other hand, did not possess the same speaking skills. He didn't particularly enjoy giving speeches, and he felt awkward reading from a teleprompter. Sometimes he would appear confused or even angry in the middle of a speech. Once, the wind blew a page of his script away without McCain noticing, and he continued his speech, not even realizing he had skipped an entire page.

Additionally, McCain did not have some of the obvious appeal that Obama had. Obama was young, attractive, and different from any presidential candidate people had ever seen— because of his biracial heritage and also his fresh approach.

In a word, the McCain campaign felt threatened.

McCain's campaign manager and staff worked hard to portray Obama as someone too inexperienced to be president. "Obama is just not *presidential*," they said. In particular, they tried to convince voters that he did not have enough international experience, the same strategy Hillary Clinton had used in the primaries. The fact that Obama had not travelled to the war zone countries as a presidential candidate (McCain had) was something that the McCain camp liked to talk about to the press.

As a result, Obama decided to travel to Europe and the Middle East in late July, 2008. Obama said he planned to meet with troops and commanders to gather information that could influence decisions he might make as president. The Obama campaign referred to the travels as a "fact-finding trip." The McCain campaign called it something else.

"This is nothing more than one giant photo opportunity for Obama," one McCain aide said in an irritated voice on Fox TV's *Morning Show*.

"McCain goes to Iraq, and the press makes fun of him," McCain's campaign manager said angrily to *Newsweek*. Then he added sarcastically, "Obama goes to Europe, and two hundred reporters go along to write about the history-making Save America's Reputation Tour."

Obama paid no attention to the McCain camp's remarks. By ignoring the comments, he made them seem whiny and childish. To make matters worse, John McCain didn't necessarily agree with his campaign manager or aides.

"I think it's great that Obama's going to Iraq and Afghanistan," McCain told reporters, much to the distress of his manager. It was not the first time, nor the last, that McCain would disagree with his aides and advisers.

When the press covered every speech and made a point of showing record-setting crowds turning out for Obama in Europe, the McCain campaign decided it was time for politics as usual. Again, in fairness, McCain himself was not a big fan of running attack ads against his opponent. However, he let his staff do what they thought was best, and the staff made some poor choices.

"He's the biggest celebrity in the world," an announcer proclaimed, while film of crowds chanting "Obama!" alternated with quick shots of Britney Spears and Paris Hilton. As dramatic music played in the background, the voice asked ominously, *"But is he ready to lead?"*

The "celebrity ad" probably did McCain more harm than good. Late-night TV hosts laughed at it. Paris Hilton mocked the commercial with one of her own, in which she referred to McCain as an "old white-haired dude." And though Obama refused to stoop to name-calling, he did say, "What they're trying to do is make you scared of me. You know, I've got a funny name. I don't look like all those other presidents on those dollar bills. I'm risky."

Immediately, the McCain campaign accused Obama of "playing the race card," meaning that Obama was saying that the McCain camp was questioning his ability to lead only because he was black. This seemed, to many Americans, to be too much of a stretch. People were weary of political bickering, and more and more of them were being drawn to this unusual candidate who refused to bicker, who moved on smoothly and confidently, who spoke of change.

And as the summer days passed, Obama took the lead.

• • •

The Democratic National Convention took place in Denver, Colorado, from August 25th to 28th. On the last day of the convention, Obama would officially accept his party's nomination for president. It had been an incredible journey from the day at the same convention, only four years ago, that Obama, virtually unknown then, gave the keynote address. Now, millions of people worldwide followed Obama's progress. In Kenya, he had become a national hero.

Obama worked very hard on his acceptance speech, staying up all night more than once to get the words just right. Throughout the convention, dozens of people gave speeches, from Michelle Obama to governors and senators to Obama's sister, Maya, to many, many everyday people. More and more, it was becoming clear that Obama's appeal to the "everyday American" was the true strength of the campaign. The idea that in the United States, "we are one"—not just a collection of opposing groups—appealed immensely to voters. And that appeal was pushing a young African American senator from Illinois, whose name had been unknown to a third of Americans only nine months earlier, closer to the White House every day.

Although the earlier events of the convention had been held in a conference center in downtown Denver, the festivities were moved outside to Mile High Stadium for the night of Obama's speech. The stage had been designed to look like an ancient Greek temple, with towering white columns and very bright lights. Some Republicans made fun of the stage, claiming that it was a ridiculous glorification of Obama, "The One."

"It's all about him," one Republican said with a laugh to an interviewer. "He's just a big star coming out on his big stage. Obamamania's in full swing."

Obama and his campaign manager took one look at the stage decoration and agreed that it was excessive. Before the speech that night, it was toned down, and the bright lights were slightly dimmed. Then, on the 45th anniversary of Martin Luther King's "I Have a Dream" speech, Obama stood in front of 80,000 people and spoke. He laid out his plan for the presidency. He clearly described the differences between himself and his opponent: "I don't believe that Senator McCain doesn't care what's going on in the lives of Americans. I just think he doesn't know. Why else would he define middle-class as someone making under five million dollars a year?"

Most importantly, Obama drove home the fact that we, as a nation, as one, shape and change our own futures. The future is not up to the president; it's up to the people.

"I stand before you tonight because all across America something is stirring. What the naysayers don't understand is that this election has never been about me. It's been about you. . . . That's the promise of America—the idea that we are responsible for ourselves, but that we also rise or fall as one nation; the fundamental belief that I am my brother's keeper; I am my sister's keeper. That's the promise we need to keep. That's the change we need right now."

• • •

Obama had chosen Joe Biden, the senior senator from Delaware, as his vice-presidential running mate. Biden had a great deal of foreign policy experience, and he was thought of as a "regular guy," someone who would appeal to blue-collar workers. Many political observers still felt that Obama would not be popular with white working-class voters, a significant part of the American public. Obama hoped that Joe Biden would help sway some voters who were still undecided.

John McCain, however, waited until the morning after Obama's acceptance speech to announce his running mate. It was widely believed that he did so intentionally to shift the focus quickly back to the Republicans the night after Obama's biggest moment in the campaign.

"Sarah Palin? Who's that?" Biden asked Obama on the morning of August 29. It was a question many people across the country were asking. McCain had taken a risk and chosen the relatively unknown young governor of Alaska. It was a risk that some of McCain's aides did not completely support. However, McCain saw his outspoken, confident, attractive running mate as the last chance to draw attention away from Barack Obama.

And for a while, it worked.

"What's the difference between a hockey mom and a pit bull?" Palin asked the crowd when she was introduced by McCain. "Lipstick!"

A self-proclaimed "hockey mom" turned politician, Palin came across as a no-nonsense conservative who could both hunt moose and balance a state budget. She was an energetic speaker who could get a crowd going. Suddenly, everyone wanted to see Sarah Palin, and the crowds she drew for McCain were as big as Obama's. Some felt she had turned McCain's campaign around.

"No Drama Obama" and his staff took a deep breath and hoped that the fascination with Palin would pass. It would have to pass quickly; Election Day was only eight weeks away. But as the next few weeks went by, Americans became less fascinated with Palin and more concerned with whether or not she could actually lead the country if she had to.

Some people were alarmed by Palin's lack of international knowledge and experience. Various interviews (particularly one with Katie Couric) revealed that Palin didn't even know what a vice president actually does. Then, Palin made matters worse by making several careless comments. At one point, she attempted to polish her international image by saying that she could see Russia from her house in Alaska (she couldn't). Another time, she referred to Africa as a country (it's a continent). Obama and his staff were careful not to attack Palin personally, but late-night comedians, talk-show hosts, and, often, the press took aim. By the time the Palin and Biden debate rolled around on October 2, the second wind that Palin had given the McCain campaign was quickly dying down.

• • •

"In the public polls that followed the first debate between Obama and McCain, Obama emerged as the winner," claimed *Newsweek* magazine. "Obama remained the cool and steady one." In the three presidential debates leading up to Election Day, this coolness and steadiness would be the key for Barack Obama. McCain often paced, grew flustered, or became short-tempered with his opponent. He was reluctant to look Obama in the eye. He avoided questions.

In rehearsals for the debates, Obama had one of his aides act as McCain. Sometimes the aide, pretending to be McCain, would try so hard to get Obama angry that both Obama and his aide would practically collapse in laughter. In the end, however, the practice worked. Obama vowed not to yell, raise his voice, or interrupt his opponent. If McCain wanted to try to provoke Obama, Obama would not take the bait. He would defend himself, but he would not join in the mudslinging.

By the time the second debate approached, nearly all of McCain's television ads had become negative. The increasing attempt to frighten voters away from Obama, however, seemed to backfire. If anything, *Newsweek* magazine pointed out, the ads led the press to "increasingly paint McCain as a bitter old man." In turn, many voters who had been undecided were beginning to support Obama.

Following the second debate, most polls showed Obama to be the clear winner. Again, he had remained cool and thoughtful. In fact, many people now referred to him as "presidential." On the other hand, a *New York Times* writer described McCain as " . . . extremely erratic. Sometimes he was too aggressive (referring to Obama as 'that one.') Other times, he just couldn't answer the questions. And his random attempts at jokes were just bad."

• • •

"Mr. Obama will raise taxes. He'll raise taxes on ordinary, everyday folks like Joe the Plumber," McCain repeated several times in the third and final debate on October 15, only three weeks away from Election Day. It was McCain's final attempt to frighten blue-collar voters away from Obama. "Joe the Plumber" was a man who, at a rally in Ohio, had questioned Obama about his small-business tax plan, worried that he'd be taxed too much. Their conversation had been aired over and over on various news channels.

McCain jumped on the opportunity to use "Joe" as a symbol of the middle class. "Joe" and the unfair taxes he might have to pay became the focus of the debate. According to MSNBC, "'Joe' was mentioned 25 times. Twenty-one times by McCain; four times by Obama. The economy was mentioned 16 times, Iraq four times." Still, Obama remained unruffled, confidently explaining how his tax plan would, in fact, help small business owners and middle-class Americans.

Only a few days after the debate, it was discovered that "Joe the Plumber" was not Joe the Plumber at all. His real name was Sam Wurzelbacher. He was not even a licensed plumber. Additionally, he actually *owed* unpaid taxes. Television, radio, and the press buzzed with the question of whether "Joe" had been a set-up all along.

If the McCain staffers had been hoping that "Joe the Plumber" would turn the tide in the final debate, they had to be disappointed. He had just the opposite effect. Obama was declared the winner of the third and final round of debates. It was, some felt, his knockout punch.

•　•　•

In the final days leading up to the national election on Tuesday, November 4, Obama warned his staff not to be overly confident.

"I've been in these positions before when we were favored, and then the press starts getting carried away and we end up getting spanked," Obama said. Like Abraham Lincoln, Obama believed that one of the most important qualities a leader could have was humility. Even so, Obama sensed that victory was, perhaps, within reach. On his last morning of campaigning, November 3, he looked out at a crowd in Florida and said, "I have just one word for you, Florida: *Tomorrow*! We have a righteous wind at our backs!"

That same day, Michelle called Barack with sad news; his grandmother, Toot, had passed away in Hawaii. Late that afternoon, Barack attended a final rally in North Carolina. Standing in front of 25,000 supporters, Obama did something he had never done before in public—he broke down and cried. Wiping the tears off his face, he spoke in a hoarse voice, "She was a silent hero, very humble and plain-spoken. She has gone home, so there's great joy as well as tears."

• • •

Obama returned to Chicago for Election Day. In the morning, he voted and then paid a surprise visit to a phone bank canvassing center, where volunteers were calling people to urge them to vote. Obama surprised a few voters by calling them himself. However, he was not allowed to campaign officially on Election Day. All he and his staff could do now was to wait for the votes to be counted.

On the afternoon of November 4, Barack Obama followed a tradition he had followed before every election. He played a pick-up basketball game with friends and staffers. That evening, Obama enjoyed a quiet dinner with his family at home while thousands of people streamed into Chicago's Grant Park for what everyone hoped would be Obama's victory speech. Later that evening, a call came in from Obama's campaign manager. Obama had won Ohio—a very important win in what was known as a "key battleground state."

"It looks like we're going to win this thing, huh?" Obama asked calmly.

"It looks like it, yeah," his campaign manager replied, doing his best to remain equally calm.

A few hours later, it was all over. Barack Obama had won.

In Grant Park, nearly half a million supporters chanted "Yes We Can!" while eagerly awaiting Obama's arrival. Before Obama even walked onstage with his family, many in the crowd were in tears. Mingling with the thousands of everyday people were Oprah Winfrey, film director Spike Lee, and Reverend Jesse Jackson. Jackson, who had been at Martin Luther King's side on the day he was killed in Memphis, wept openly as Obama said, "What began twenty-one months ago in the depths of winter must not end on this autumn night."

• • •

All across the United States, people celebrated a day that many had believed they would never live to see: the day an African American was elected president. In the remote

Kenyan village Obama had come to know as "Home Squared" so many years ago, relatives hugged and shouted, "We are going to the White House! We are going to the White House!" And, truly, around the entire world, from the Eiffel Tower in Paris to the halls of Obama's old elementary school in Indonesia, shouts of victory echoed.

Barack Obama stood on the stage in Grant Park that evening, waving and smiling, waiting for the thunderous cheers of the crowd to die down. It had been quite a journey—from his unusual heritage as the son of a white American woman and an African man, to a childhood split between Indonesia and Hawaii, to the sometimes troubled soul-searching of youth, the years at Harvard, the community activism, the work as a senator, and finally to the White House. Some would call the journey improbable. Others, before this night, would have called it impossible.

"If there is anyone out there who still doubts that America is a place where all things are possible," Barack Obama, 44th President of the United States, began his victory speech that night, "who still wonders if the dream of our founders is alive in our time; who still questions the power of our democracy, tonight is your answer. . . . It's been a long time coming, but tonight, because of what we did on this day, in this election, at this defining moment, change has come to America."

• • •

In so many ways, the journey to change was just beginning.

# EPILOGUE:
# THE INAUGURATION

Sasha and Malia Obama stood with their parents inside the Lincoln Memorial in Washington, D.C. It was a week and a half before Inauguration Day, to be held on January 20th, 2009. Michelle and Barack had decided to take their girls on a "field trip" to see some of the monuments around the city. After all, this city would be the family's home for at least the next four years.

Obama was particularly interested in having his girls see the Lincoln Memorial. It had been upon the steps of this memorial, in 1963, that Martin Luther King had delivered his "I Have a Dream" speech. It had been Abraham Lincoln who had worked tirelessly, as our nation's sixteenth president, to end slavery. And it was to Lincoln's wisdom, humility, and love of country that Obama often looked for direction and inspiration.

Seven-year-old Sasha stared up at the impressive statue of Abraham Lincoln. Lincoln's face looked serious, almost worried, but kind.

On the towering north wall, the words from Lincoln's Second Inaugural Address were engraved in marble. Sasha gazed at them for a bit and then looked up at her father.

"Will you be giving a speech like that, Daddy?" she asked.

Barack smiled at his youngest daughter and looked up at the words.

*With malice toward none, with charity for all, with firmness in the right as God gives us to see the right, let us strive on to finish the work we are in, to bind up the nation's wounds.*

It was a touching moment, but ten-year-old Malia was already thinking ahead. She folded her arms and nodded at her father. "First African American president—it better be good."

Later, Obama related this story to the press, adding with a laugh, "So I just want you all to know the pressures I'm under here from my children."

• • •

Four days before the inauguration, Obama and his family boarded a train in Philadelphia. They would be following a portion of the same "whistle stop" trip that Abraham Lincoln had taken on the way to his first inauguration in 1861. The train would stop in Philadelphia; Wilmington, Delaware (to pick up Joe Biden); Baltimore, Maryland; and then end in Washington, D.C. Along the way, Obama would make speeches and stand outside to wave to those who would not be able to attend the inaugural festivities—exactly as Lincoln had done. Obama and Biden wanted to show their appreciation to the everyday Americans who had supported them. In fact, with them on the train were forty-one people from fifty states, all of them representing everyday America. One of them, Rosa Mendoza, a 54-year-old English teacher from Las Vegas, stepped aboard the train with tears in her eyes.

"It is like a dream," Mendoza said as the train left the station. "I hardly know how to describe it."

Then, as the old-fashioned train traveled along, Mendoza looked out at people lining the tracks from Philadelphia to Washington. People of all races and backgrounds waved, cheered, and held signs congratulating the new president. Three times, the train stopped so that the president-elect could speak. Mostly, Obama told the stories of the everyday people aboard—including Rosa Mendoza's. Mendoza was a single mother who had worked at two waitressing jobs to take care of her daughter and put herself through college. It was difficult, but she had never failed to believe that America is a land of opportunity where anything is possible if one works hard. In Barack Obama, she had found someone who, she said, "understood my world."

"These are the stories that will drive me in the days ahead," Obama said to the crowds.

That evening, as the train rolled into Washington, Mendoza smiled. Finally, she found the words to express what she was feeling. "It is like the angels have poured bliss on me," she said.

• • •

January 20 dawned cold and clear. However, long before the sun rose on the National Mall, the two-mile-long park that stretches from the Capitol to the Lincoln Memorial, the crowds began forming. Barack Obama would not be sworn in until noon; but before dawn, the Washington subways were jammed with those making their way to the Mall.

By nine in the morning, more than a half million people had gathered. By eleven, some estimated the record-setting crowd to be close to two million people. It was a mass of humanity big enough to be seen from outer space. There had never been a larger crowd gathered at our nation's Capitol.

"Obama! Obama! Obama!"

The chant rolled like a wave from the steps of the Lincoln Memorial to the steps of the Capitol and then back again. With more than a million voices raised, some later said that it felt like thunder shaking the very ground they stood upon. And although thousands of police officers, Secret Service agents, and National Guardsmen swarmed the area near the Capitol, there were few disturbances.

"As far as you can see, everyone has the same expression," one reporter said. "It's more than celebration, more than gaiety. People are *happy*—so happy for this day."

As the noon hour grew closer, hundreds of thousands of American flags were held high. And when it was announced that it was time for Obama to take the presidential oath of office, every flag waved wildly, turning the National Mall into a sea of vibrating red, white, and blue. Many news announcers pointed out that they had not seen so many flags or witnessed so much pride and patriotism since the days following the 9/11 attacks.

As Barack Obama stepped forward with Michelle and his daughters by his side, a roar erupted from the vast crowd. Then, just as quickly, a hush fell over those gathered to watch this historic moment. At Obama's special request, Abraham Lincoln's own Bible was used for the oath. It was the first time the burgundy velvet Bible had made an appearance since Lincoln himself had used it for his second inauguration in 1865. With Michelle holding the Bible, Obama placed his left hand on it, raised his right hand, and repeated these words:

*I, Barack Hussein Obama, do solemnly swear that I will faithfully execute the office of President of the United States, and will to the best of my ability, preserve, protect and defend the Constitution of the United States. So help me God.*

As the twenty-one-gun salute boomed, people cheered, but just as many cried.

"It's been a long time coming," an older African American woman said, tears covering her face. "I remember well the day Dr. King died. I said to myself, 'What about his dream?' Well, today, right now, right here in this very place, Martin Luther King's dream has just come true."

Following the swearing-in ceremony, Obama delivered his inaugural address.

"That we are in the midst of crisis is now well understood. Our nation is at war, against a far-reaching network of violence and hatred. Our economy is badly weakened," Obama stated. Then he called on the American people for humility, gratitude, and sacrifice as the way to overcome the bad times.

"Starting today, we must pick ourselves up, dust ourselves off, and begin again the work of remaking America," Obama urged. He was echoing the sentiments of Abraham Lincoln who had said, as he entered the presidency in the midst of crisis, "We must think anew and act anew."

When Barack Obama finished his address, the nation, and the world, celebrated.

In the Civil Rights Museum in Memphis, Tennessee, blacks and whites held hands and repeated "Yes we can!"

In Belfast, Ireland, newspapers rushed to print the headlines: "Obama: Dawn of a New Era."

In Baghdad, a six-and-a-half-foot African American soldier smiled broadly at a camera as tears fell on his cheeks.

In the streets of Nairobi, Kenya, people danced and hugged.

And on the Capitol steps, steps that slaves had once worked to build, little Sasha Obama looked up at her father and grinned. Giving him a thumbs-up sign, she said, "Daddy, you're now officially the president!"